The Complete Films of Humphrey Bogart

The Complete Films of

HUMPHREY BOGART

by Clifford McCarty

CITADEL PRESS   **SECAUCUS, N.J.**

ACKNOWLEDGMENTS

Grateful acknowledgment is made to the many individuals who extended their help to the author during the preparation of this book.

For their most generous loan of photographs and for other assistance, my special thanks go to Homer Dickens and Gene Ringgold, whose unfailing cooperation literally made this book possible.

For their various courtesies, my thanks go also to Rudy Behlmer, Louis Bensussen, Barbara Browning, Carlos Clarens, Lloyd Cohn, Warren Dawson, William Edgar, Hal Findlay, Ozzie Graner, Bob McKinney, Joseph McLaughlin, William F. Nolan, Ed Plantamura, Ray Polson, Lillian Schwartz, Mildred Simpson, and Miss Joan Blondell.

Published by Citadel Press
A division of Lyle Stuart Inc.
120 Enterprise Ave., Secaucus, N.J. 07094
In Canada: Musson Book Company
A division of General Publishing Co. Limited
Don Mills, Ontario
Manufactured in the United States of America
ISBN 0-8065-0955-4

Originally published as *Bogey: The Films of Humphrey Bogart*

Contents

Introduction

Humphrey Bogart appeared in seventy-five feature films.[1] The very number surprises many people, even avowed fans. But in his busiest period, from 1936 to 1940, Bogart was amassing an impressive number of credits, averaging one picture every two months. By the time he made *High Sierra*—perhaps the first of the films now considered to be "Bogart pictures"—half of his films were behind him. They were, for the most part, forgettable films—"shaky-A," "B," and even "C" pictures—though a few were notable: *Black Legion, Dead End, Angels With Dirty Faces, The Roaring Twenties.* In most of them he had only supporting roles, frequently the gangster parts that earned him a reputation as the screen's "No. 1 Bad Boy."

Success did not come early. He was thirty-one when he made his first movie, thirty-seven when *The Petrified Forest* secured his position as a film actor. Prob-

ably because of the tough-guy roles he so often played, many thought his origin was New York's Lower East Side. Actually he came from the comfortable upper West Side, the son of Dr. Belmont DeForest Bogart, a distinguished surgeon, and Maud Humphrey Bogart, a noted magazine illustrator. Said Bogart, "There wasn't a drop of theatrical blood in me."

He was born on January 23, 1899. (Warner publicity later changed his birthdate to December 25, 1900, possibly to foster the view that a man born on Christmas Day couldn't really be as villainous as he appeared on the screen.) The Bogarts were well-to-do and lived in a big brownstone house just off West End Avenue. Next door lived William A. Brady, the theatrical producer, whose son Bill and Bogart were childhood playmates. After attending Trinity School in New York, Bogart was sent to Phillips Academy at Andover, Massachusetts,

to prepare for Yale. His independent spirit asserted itself, however, and he was expelled for a schoolboy prank. When the United States entered World War I, Bogart joined the Navy, serving aboard the troopship *Leviathan,* where he received the wood splinter that permanently scarred his lip.

After the war Bogart approached Brady for work, and the producer made him office boy, later an assistant company manager, and finally stage manager at Brady's New York studio, World Film Corporation. It was there that Bogart's first venture into films took place. Brady was producing a picture called *Life,* with Arline Pretty and Rod LaRocque. Toward the end of production, Brady discharged the director and told Bogart to finish the thing. "I did a fine job," Bogart recalled. "There were some beautiful shots of people walking along the streets, with me in the window making wild gestures. There was an automobile chase scene in which a car ran into itself. So Mr. Brady stepped in and directed the rest of it himself."

Brady next put him to work at fifty dollars a week as a road company manager, and in 1920, on tour with *The "Ruined" Lady,* he made his initial stage appearance. Said Bogart: "I went on the stage the first time as a gag. I'd been kidding Neil Hamilton about the soft life of an actor. 'Acting doesn't look very hard to me,' I'd said. The funny thing was that that was what I actually thought. The last night of the play, he dared me to go on in his place. I took the dare, and it was all a horrible fiasco. In one scene, an actor was supposed to be mad at me, and I thought he was really mad; he scared the hell out of me. It was the first time I had been face to face with actors at work. I didn't realize how convincing they could be. After that experience, I thought, 'Never again.' What changed my mind was finding out I'd never get rich as a stage manager. I was young and I wanted to get ahead in the world, so I went to Mr. Brady and told him my problem. He said, 'Why don't you become an actor? Actors earn good money.' So, to make a fortune, I became an actor."

Early in 1922 he appeared in *Drifting,* and later the same year he won the second lead in *Swifty,* Alexander Woollcott's review of which Bogart was reputed to have carried with him thereafter. Wrote Woollcott for all the world and Bogart to read: "The young man who embodies the sprig is what is usually and mercifully described as inadequate."

But Bogart kept acting and gradually learned his craft. He usually was cast as romantic juveniles, his stage equipment a tennis racquet and a pair of flannels. Among his plays were *Meet the Wife* (1923), *Nerves* (1924), *Hell's Bells* and *Cradle Snatchers* (1925), *Baby Mine* (1927), *Saturday's Children* (1928), and *Skyrocket* and *It's a Wise Child* (1929).[2]

Bogart's screen debut, in a lowly short subject called *Broadway's Like That,* was something less than auspicious. Indeed it was unknown, or at least forgotten, until 1963, when it was discovered during the research for David L. Wolper's television production, *The Man Called Bogart.* Two rare stills from *Broadway's Like That,* believed to be the first ever published, appear in this book.

Spotted by Fox scouts in *It's a Wise Child,* Bogart went to Hollywood in 1930 and was signed at four hundred dollars a week. He made five pictures for Fox and one, on loanout, for Universal. There was an attempt at first to turn him into a sort of rugged glamour boy; at the end he was made a cowboy. Said Bogart succinctly: "I spent a very unsuccessful year at Fox." He returned to New York, convinced that the stage was his medium.

The country was in the grip of the Depression, and Broadway was experiencing one of its worst seasons. While appearing in *After All* (1931), he succumbed to Columbia Pictures' offer of a six-month contract and withdrew from the play, but during this time he made only one film. He then went to Warners for two pictures, after which he went back to New York a second time, swearing never to return to Hollywood. He appeared in four more plays: *I Loved You Wednesday* and *Chrysalis* (1932) and *Our Wife* and *The Mask and the Face* (1933), followed by a picture made in New York called *Midnight.*

In 1934 Bogart opened in the play *Invitation to a Murder.* "Arthur Hopkins, the producer, came to see the show," recalled Bogart. "He remembered me in it. A few months later, when he was getting ready to produce *The Petrified Forest,* he sent for me. When I dropped into his office, Robert E. Sherwood—who wrote the play and who was a friend of mine—was there. Hopkins said to me, 'I've got a good role for you. A gangster role.' Sherwood spoke up and said, 'Why, you must be crazy. He doesn't fit that part at all! What he ought to do is the part of the football player.' They argued back and forth, and I thought Sherwood was right. I couldn't picture myself playing a gangster. So what happened? I made a hit as the gangster."

The star of *The Petrified Forest* was Leslie Howard, and the play was an instant success. Bogart and Howard became friends, and Howard promised that if the play were made into a picture, he would try to bring Bogart along to repeat his role on the screen. "When Warners bought the screen rights and signed up Leslie Howard," Bogart wrote, "they tested several actors for the Mantee part and finally settled on Edward G. Robinson, who had won a reputation in tough-guy roles. Unhappy about this, I cabled Leslie, who was in Scotland, and he promptly informed the studio that if I didn't play Mantee, he would not play either. So I got the job."

He signed a contract with Warner Bros. and was launched on the screen's most celebrated career of

menace. He was featured in a long series of crime pictures, prompting one reviewer to write that "guns and Bogart go together like July and Jap beetles." Occasionally, as in *Stand-In* and *Dark Victory,* he was given a chance to act without a gun up his sleeve, but usually he was cast as the heavy, by picture's end dead or in prison. During his years in gangster parts he fought continually with Jack L. Warner for better roles, not unaware that most of those assigned him were beneath his ability.

"I'm known as the guy who always squawks about roles, but never refuses to play one," he once said. "I've never forgotten a piece of advice Holbrook Blinn gave me when I was a young squirt and asked him how I could get a reputation as an actor. He said, 'Just keep working.' The idea is that if you're always busy, sometime somebody is going to get the idea that you must be good." He even culled a certain amount of enjoyment from his type casting: "When the heavy, full of crime and bitterness, grabs his wounds and talks about death and taxes in a husky voice, the audience is his and his alone."

Bogart's career reached a turning-point with *High Sierra.* He was still a gangster, but this time a sympathetic one, and the public demanded to see more of the dynamic man who was a real actor. With his next picture, *The Wagons Roll at Night,* Bogart received top billing, and thereafter never got anything less. In 1941 he brought private-eye Sam Spade brilliantly to life in the "sleeper" of the year—*The Maltese Falcon.* Perfectly cast, with John Huston's taut script and direction, it remains to this day the finest mystery film ever made. One more picture like the *Falcon* was all Bogart needed.

What he got was *Casablanca.* Warners' masterly production, the work of Bogart and the stunning cast, and the incredible timeliness of the picture made it one of the biggest money-makers in the company's history. With *Casablanca,* Bogart reached a level of popularity that he maintained for seven years: from 1943 to 1949 he ranked among the top ten money-making stars. In 1945 he married his leading lady in *To Have and Have Not,* Lauren Bacall, after a well-publicized courtship.[3] Their second film together, *The Big Sleep,* was advertised as "the picture they were born for."

Bogart was now at the peak of his popularity and was the highest-paid actor in the world. In 1947 he formed his own company, Santana Pictures, and made four films as his own employee. In 1948 he starred in John Huston's memorable allegory of greed, riches and disaster, *The Treasure of the Sierra Madre.* He received high praise from the critics for his performance as the paranoid prospector, but the public resented his change of character. He returned to the familiar Bogart role in *Key Largo,* one of his most successful films. It may even be said to be the last of the "Bogart pictures"

in the sense that the character he played fell into the mold established by *Casablanca.*

The 1950s saw a somewhat different Bogart—more mature, less frequently type-cast. If some of his films caused a nostalgia for the old Bogey, others commanded respect for the wider range they afforded his talents. The moody screenwriter of *In a Lonely Place,* the seedy rumpot of *The African Queen,* the neurotic martinet of *The Caine Mutiny,* the veteran director of *The Barefoot Contessa* were all memorable characterizations. In 1955 his name once again appeared among the top ten box office champions.

In March, 1956, as his last picture, *The Harder They Fall,* went into release, Bogart underwent an operation for cancer of the esophagus. The disease spread, however, and finally, at 2:10 on the morning of January 14, 1957, he died in his sleep at his home in Los Angeles.

Behind him was a legacy that few are privileged to leave—a legacy of motion pictures to be seen and remembered, and seen again. They all have interest, if only because Bogart is in them. A dozen or so are very good indeed, and at least one—*The Treasure of the Sierra Madre*—is among the greatest films ever made. "All he has to do to dominate a scene is to enter it," wrote Raymond Chandler; and, through revivals in threatres and on television, the screen is still filled—as it was for two decades—with his enormous presence.

[1] He also made two short subjects, two trailers, and three unbilled guest appearances, all of which are covered in this book.

[2] In 1957, *Variety* wrote that Bogart "finally got work in some of the silent films made around New York," but this unsubstantiated assertion has never, to my knowledge, been verified.

[3] He had been married three times before, to actresses Helen Menken (1926-27), Mary Phillips (1928-37), and Mayo Methot (1938-45).

The Complete Films of Humphrey Bogart

As Dobbs in *The Treasure of the Sierra Madre*

With Ruth Etting

Broadway's Like That
1930

Vitaphone Varieties No. 960. Produced by the Vita-phone Corporation. Distributed by Warner Bros. Director-in-chief, Murray Roth. Story and dialogue by Stanley Rauh. Musical director, Harold Levey. Running time, 10 minutes.

CAST

Ruth Etting, Humphrey Bogart, Joan Blondell.

This short, made in New York, was Bogart's first picture. In the scenes shown here, Bogart is having lunch with Miss Etting in a restaurant called Lee Sing Chop Suey. This sequence is preceded by the title, "There's nothing sweeter than lunch with a sweetie."

Wrote *Motion Picture News:* "Ruth Etting may have a good 'blue' voice for stage reproduction but it isn't so hot when placed for 'mike' reception. Ruth is placed here in a short dramatic setting showing the city slicker up to his old tricks. She breaks out into song when she should be weeping. However, Broadway's like that."

With Ruth Etting

A Devil With Women

1930

A Fox Picture. Directed by Irving Cummings. Associate producer, George Middleton. Screenplay by Dudley Nichols and Henry M. Johnson. Based on the novel Dust and Sun *by Clements Ripley. Director of photography, Arthur Todd. Music by Peter Brunelli. Film editor, Jack Murray. Art director, William Darling. Sound recorders, E. Clayton Ward and Harry M. Leonard. Song, "Amor Mio," by James Monaco and Cliff Friend. Running time, 76 minutes.*

CAST

Jerry Maxton	VICTOR MCLAGLEN
Rosita Fernandez	Mona MARIS
Tom Standish	Humphrey BOGART
Dolores	Luana Alcaniz
Morloff	Michael Vavitch
Jiminez	Soledad Jiminez
Alicia	Mona Rico
Don Diego	John St. Polis
General Garcia	Robert Edeson

SYNOPSIS

Jerry Maxton, a soldier of fortune stranded in a Central American banana republic, is hired to end the activities of Morloff, a notorious bandit. He is hounded along the way by Tom Standish, nephew of the richest power in the country, who tags along for a lark.

Jerry, though hungering for women and battle, gets only the latter. He falls for a woman gun-smuggler who lures him into Morloff's camp, where he and Tom narrowly escape a firing squad. They take refuge in the hacienda of Rosita Fernandez. When the bandits attempt an assault on the hacienda, Rosita entices them inside one at a time, and Jerry demolishes them in a series of one-punch fights. The battle over and Morloff killed, Jerry believes Rosita is his, but Tom proves to be the señorita's choice.

With Mona Maris

With Victor McLaglen and Mona Maris

With Mona Maris

With Spencer Tracy

Up the River
1930

A Fox Picture. Directed by John Ford. Original screenplay by Maurine Watkins. Director of photography, Joseph August. Staged by William Collier, Sr. Film editor, Frank Hull. Sound recorder, W. W. Lindsay, Jr. Running time, 92 minutes.

With Claire Luce

CAST

St. Louis	Spencer TRACY
Judy	Claire LUCE
Dannemora Dan	Warren HYMER
Steve	Humphrey BOGART
Pop	William COLLIER, SR.
Jean	Joan Marie Lawes
Jessup	George MacFarlane
Morris	Gaylord Pendleton
Edith LaVerne	Sharon Lynn
Sophie	Noel Francis
Kit	Goodee Montgomery
Slim	Robert Burns
Clem	John Swor
The Warden	Robert E. O'Connor
Mrs. Massey	Louise MacIntosh
Dick	Richard Keene
Happy	Johnnie Walker
Beauchamp	Pat Somerset
Frosby	Morgan Wallace
Mrs. Jordan	Edythe Chapman
Cynthia	Althea Henly
May and June	Keating Sisters
Deputy Warden	Joe Brown
Whiteley	Wilbur Mack
Nash	Harvey Clark
Daisy Elmore	Carol Wines
Minnie	Adele Windsor
Annie	Mildred Vincent

With Claire Luce, Spencer Tracy,
and Warren Hymer,

SYNOPSIS

Two escaped convicts, St. Louis and Dannemora Dan, have a falling out, are apprehended, and are sent back to prison. Also in prison, serving a sentence for accidental manslaughter, is Steve, whose respectable New England parents think he is in China. In the women's wing of the penitentiary is Judy, framed by a crooked stock salesman named Frosby. Steve and Judy fall in love, and when Steve comes up for parole he promises to wait for Judy.

Frosby, hearing of the romance, follows Steve to his home and threatens to expose him as a jailbird unless Steve helps him fleece the townspeople. Judy learns of this in prison and confides in St. Louis and Danny, who take it upon themselves to help the young couple. During the prison's theatrical show, St. Louis and Danny escape in feminine costumes and go to New England to thwart Frosby's plans. Their job finished, they return to prison in time to win the annual baseball game for their alma mater.

With Claire Luce

With Warren Hymer and Spencer Tracy

With Donald Dillaway and Charles Farrell

With Goodes Montgomery, Charles Farrell,
and Donald Dillaway

With Charles Farrell

Body and Soul
1931

A Fox Picture. Directed by Alfred Santell. Screenplay by Jules Furthman. From the play Squadrons *by A. E. Thomas, based on the story "Big Eyes and Little Mouth" by Elliott White Springs. Director of photography, Glen MacWilliams. Music by Peter Brunelli. Film editor, Paul Weatherwax. Art director, Anton Grot. Special effects by Ralph Hammeras. Sound recorder, Donald Flick. Technical adviser, Bogart Rogers. Running time, 83 minutes.*

CAST

Mal Andrews	CHARLES FARRELL
Carla	ELISSA LANDI
Jim Watson	Humphrey BOGART
Alice Lester	Myrna LOY
Tap Johnson	Donald Dillaway
Major Burke	Craufurd Kent
Major Knowls	Pat Somerset
General Trafford-Jones	Ian MacLaren
Lieutenant Meggs	Dennis D'Auburn
Zane	Douglas Dray
Young	Harold Kinney
Sam Douglas	Bruce Warren

SYNOPSIS

During World War I, several American flyers, including Mal Andrews, Jim Watson, and Tap Johnson, are attached to a Royal Air Force squadron in France. Watson, married a few days before sailing, has since picked up a girl friend in England. Watson is killed while attacking a German observation balloon, but Andrews, who has sneaked along on the flight, destroys the balloon and sees that Watson receives posthumous credit for the success of the attack.

On leave in England, Andrews attempts to return the watch and letters that Watson had received from a girl called "Pom-Pom." A newspaper ad brings a girl named Carla to the inn where Andrews is staying. Andrews assumes she is Watson's girl friend. Carla doesn't correct his impression, and they fall in love.

Meanwhile, Allied aviators are encountering a series of misfortunes, one of which takes Johnson's life. Carla, suspected of giving information to the enemy, is accused by British Intelligence of being a spy with Andrews an accessory. Alice Lester claims to be the real "Pom-Pom," but Carla demonstrates on the basis of the letters written to Watson that she is Watson's widow and that Alice is the spy.

With Sidney Fox

With Bette Davis and Conrad Nagel

Bad Sister
1931

A Universal Picture. Directed by Hobart Henley. Produced by Carl Laemmle, Jr. Scenario by Raymond L. Schrock and Tom Reed. Dialogue by Edwin H. Knopf. Based on the story "The Flirt" by Booth Tarkington. Director of photography, Karl Freund. Film editor, Ted Kent. Sound recorder, C. Roy Hunter. Running time, 71 minutes.

CAST

Dick Lindley	Conrad Nagel
Marianne Madison	Sidney Fox
Laura Madison	Bette Davis
Minnie	ZaSu Pitts
Sam	Slim Summerville
Mr. Madison	Charles Winninger
Mrs. Madison	Emma Dunn
Valentine Corliss	Humphrey Bogart
Wade Trumbull	Bert Roach
Hedrick Madison	David Durand

SYNOPSIS

Marianne Madison, the spoiled daughter of an Indiana merchant, carries on a coquettish flirtation with Dr. Dick Lindley and regards the attentions of young Wade Trumbull with amused contempt. Bored with her suitors and small-town life and feeling that she is entitled to something more, she falls easy prey to

Valentine Corliss, a city slicker in town to swindle the local businessmen. Courting her, and beguiling her with his scheme to build a new factory, Corliss dupes Marianne into forging her father's name to a letter of endorsement which he then uses to solicit money from other merchants. Inducing Marianne to elope with him, he skips town with the money.

With Marianne gone, Laura, her quiet and unobtrusive sister, reveals to Dick that she has always loved him although knowing that he loved Marianne. Corliss deserts Marianne in a cheap hotel and she contritely returns home, but Dick has found that it is Laura whom he really loves. Marianne, who had always thought of Wade as a pleasant rustic, now sees him in a new light and accepts his proposal of marriage.

With Sidney Fox

Women of All Nations

1931

A Fox Picture. Directed by Raoul Walsh. Original screenplay by Barry Connors. Based on the characters created by Laurence Stallings and Maxwell Anderson. Director of photography, Lucien Andriot. Music by *Reginald H. Bassett. Film editor, Jack Dennis. Art director, David Hall. Sound recorder, George H. Leverett. Musical director, Carli D. Elinor. Production manager, Archibald Buchanan. Running time, 72 minutes.*

With Edmund Lowe and Victor McLaglen

CAST

Sergeant Flagg	Victor MCLAGLEN
Sergeant Quirt	Edmund LOWE
Elsa	Greta NISSEN
Olsen	El BRENDEL
Fifi	Fifi Dorsay
Pee Wee	Marjorie White
Captain of Marines	T. Roy Barnes
Prince Hassan	Bela Lugosi
Stone	Humphrey Bogart
Kiki	Joyce Compton
Izzie	Jesse DeVorska
Leon	Charles Judels
Gretchen	Marion Lessing
Ruth	Ruth Warren

SYNOPSIS

Flagg and Quirt, who have fought together in World War I and in Panama, are in Brooklyn, where Flagg is a Marine recruiting officer and Quirt runs a Turkish bath for women. When Quirt's reducing parlor is raided by the police, Flagg re-enlists Quirt in the Marines.

They go to Sweden, where they compete for the affections of Elsa, a café entertainer, but they are thrown out by Elsa's giant sweetheart, who returns home unexpectedly. Next they go to Nicaragua, where they help earthquake victims rebuild their homes.

Sent to Egypt, they again find Elsa, who now is one of the many wives of Prince Hassan. During Hassan's absence they make a play for Elsa, but when the Prince returns suddenly they flee the palace.

19

With James Kirkwood

With Rita LaRoy and Stanley Fields

With George O'Brien

A Holy Terror
1931

A Fox Picture. Directed by Irving Cummings. Associate producer, Edmund Grainger. Scenario by Ralph Block. Dialogue by Alfred A. Cohn and Myron Fagan. Based on the novel Trailin' *by Max Brand. Director of photography, George Schneiderman. Film editor, Ralph Dixon. Sound recorder, Donald Flick. Running time, 53 minutes.*

CAST

Tony Bard	George O'BRIEN
Jerry Foster	Sally EILERS
Kitty Carroll	Rita LaRoy
Steve Nash	Humphrey Bogart
William Drew	James Kirkwood
Butch Morgan	Stanley Fields
Thomas Woodbury	Robert Warwick
Tom Hedges	Richard Tucker
Jim Lawler	Earl Pingree

SYNOPSIS

Tony Bard, son of an eastern millionaire, comes in from a polo match to find his father murdered. Among his father's papers, Tony finds evidence that his name originally was not as he has known it. He also discovers the name of Drew, a Western rancher who Tony suspects may know something of his father's death.

Flying west, Tony loses control of his plane and crashes into Jerry Foster's bathroom. Jerry becomes attracted to Tony, which arouses the jealousy of her suitor, Steve Nash, foreman of the Drew ranch. Drew sends Nash and a henchman, Butch Morgan, to bring Tony in, but Tony escapes and rides to the ranch for a showdown with Drew. Morgan arrives and attempts to shoot Tony, but Drew steps between them and is wounded. Drew reveals that he is really Tony's father. He had gone east for a reckoning with the man who had stolen his wife and child many years before, and during a scuffle the supposed father had been killed when Drew's gun went off accidentally.

With Dorothy Mackaill

COURTESY OF HARVEY STEWART

Love Affair
1932

A Columbia Picture. Directed by Thornton Freeland. Adaptation and dialogue by Jo Swerling. Continuity by Dorothy Howell. Based on the College Humor *story by Ursula Parrott. Director of photography, Ted Tetzlaff. Film editor, Jack Dennis. Sound recorder, Charles Noyes. Running time, 68 minutes.*

CAST

Carol Owen	DOROTHY MACKAILL
Jim Leonard	Humphrey BOGART
Gilligan	Jack Kennedy
Felice	Barbara Leonard
Linda Lee	Astrid Allwyn
Georgie	Bradley Page
Kibbee	Halliwell Hobbes
Bruce Hardy	Hale Hamilton
Antone	Harold Minjir

SYNOPSIS

Carol Owen, a carefree young heiress, takes up flying on a whim and falls in love with her instructor, Jim Leonard, an aeronautical engineer who teaches flying while trying to promote his new airplane motor. Trying to keep up with the gay whirl of Carol's wealthy set, Jim neglects his work. They have an affair and Jim proposes, but Carol refuses, realizing that she is keeping him from fulfilling his ambitions. Jim buries himself in his work, determined to make good for Carol's sake.

Carol learns that her father left her penniless upon his death a year before, and that her financial advisor, Bruce Hardy, has been supporting her. Hardy, a perennial suitor, again proposes, and Carol accepts, with a view toward persuading him to finance Jim's invention. Jim misunderstands, rejects Hardy's aid, and casts Carol from his life.

Realizing that she loves Jim and cannot go through with the marriage, Carol goes to Hardy's home to break her engagement. Jim arrives and tells Hardy he has a personal matter to discuss with him. Thinking that Jim is going to reveal their affair, Carol angrily tells Hardy of the affair herself. But Jim has come about his sister, who has been involved in an affair with Hardy. When Jim leaves, Hardy accuses Carol of marrying him to further the career of her lover.

Feeling that she has lost Jim and that her life is futile and empty, Carol goes to the flying field to make her first and last solo flight. She leaves a note for the airport manager, and Jim learns of her plan, saving her by reaching her plane as it is about to take off.

With Evalyn Knapp, Inez Courtney
Walter Catlett, Lyle Talbot,
Sheila Terry, Ned Sparks, and
Josephine Dunn

With Inez Courtney, Joan Blondell,
Ned Sparks, Evalyn Knapp,
Lyle Talbot, and Josephine Dunn

Big City Blues
1932

A Warner Bros. Picture. Directed by Mervyn LeRoy. Screenplay by Ward Morehouse and Lillie Hayward. Based on the play New York Town *by Ward Morehouse. Director of photography, James Van Trees. Film editor, Ray Curtis. Music and arrangements by Ray Heindorf and Bernhard Kaun. Musical director, Leo F. Forbstein. Running time, 65 minutes.*

With Joan Blondell, Eric Linden,
Ned Sparks, Thomas Jackson,
Walter Catlett, Josephine Dunn,
Inez Courtney, and Evalyn Knapp

CAST

Vida	JOAN BLONDELL
Bud	Eric LINDEN
Faun	Inez Courtney
Jo-Jo	Evalyn Knapp
Hummel	Guy Kibbee
Sully	Lyle Talbot
Agnes	Gloria Shea
Gibbony	Walter Catlett
Serena	Jobyna Howland
Adkins	Humphrey Bogart
Jackie	Josephine Dunn
Station Agent	Grant Mitchell
Quelkin	Thomas Jackson
Stackhouse	Ned Sparks
Lorna	Sheila Terry
Red	Tom Dugan
Mabel	Betty Gillette
Baggage Master	Edward McWade

SYNOPSIS

Bud, inheriting some money, leaves his small Indiana town and comes to New York. On his first day in town his city cousin, Gibbony, introduces him to Vida, a chorus girl. She is nice to him and he falls for her.

With Bud's money, Gibbony throws a party in Bud's hotel room. After much drinking, a girl is killed by a bottle thrown by a drunk. Everybody flees, and Bud is suspected because the death occurred in his room.

The next evening a detective picks up Vida and Bud in a night club, but they are cleared when the killer is found a suicide. Bud takes the train back home, where he arrives just seventy-two hours after he left.

With Inez Courtney, Evalyn Knapp,
Walter Catlett, Josephine Dunn,
Sheila Terry, Ned Sparks,
Joan Blondell, and Lyle Talbot

With Allen Jenkins ,
Lyle Talbot, and Jack LaRue

Three on a Match
1932

A First National Picture for Warner Bros. Directed by Mervyn LeRoy. Scenario by Lucien Hubbard. Dialogue by Kubec Glasmon and John Bright. Based on a story by Kubec Glasmon and John Bright. Director of photography, Sol Polito. Film editor, Ray Curtis. Art director, Robert Haas. Orchestral arrangements by Ray Heindorf. Musical director, Leo F. Forbstein. Running time, 64 minutes.

CAST

Mary Keaton	Joan BLONDELL
Henry Kirkwood	Warren WILLIAM
Vivian Revere	Ann DVORAK
Ruth Westcott	Bette DAVIS
Mike Loftus	Lyle Talbot
The Mug	Humphrey Bogart
Linda	Patricia Ellis
Naomi	Sheila Terry
Principal of School	Grant Mitchell
Vivian's Chum	Glenda Farrell
Bobby	Frankie Darro
Mrs. Keaton	Clara Blandick
Defense Attorney	Hale Hamilton
Horace	Dick Brandon
Max	Junior Johnson
Vivian as a child	Anne Shirley
Mary as a child	Virginia Davis
Ruth as a child	Betty Carrs
Junior	Buster Phelps

SYNOPSIS

Ten years after graduating from public school, three girls meet again. Mary, the tomboy, has been through reform school and is now on the stage. Vivian, the snob, is married to Henry Kirkwood, a rich lawyer. Ruth, the honor student, is a business girl. Reminiscing, the girls light their cigarettes from a single match and laugh off the superstition that bad luck will befall the third person (Vivian) to use the match.

Vivian, suddenly bored with her life, decides to take her son, Junior, on an ocean cruise, and invites her girl friends to her bon voyage party. Mary arrives with a gambler, Mike Loftus, to whom Vivian is immediately attracted, and instead of sailing, she runs off with him. Kirkwood solicits Mary's help in locating his wife and son, and when he finds Vivian living with Loftus, he sues for divorce and is granted custody of the boy. He falls in love with Mary and marries her, hiring Ruth as his son's companion.

Reading of Kirkwood's second marriage, Vivian remorsefully takes to alcohol and drugs. Loftus, having lost all her money and unable to pay his gambling debts, hires "The Mug" and his henchmen to kidnap Junior. Attempting to stop them, Vivian is seized and also held captive. Knowing that she and Junior will be killed as soon as the ransom is paid, Vivian writes a message in lipstick on her nightgown and jumps from a window of the hideout. She is killed in the fall, but the message alerts the police, who apprehend the kidnappers before they can harm her son.

24

Midnight
1934

With Sidney Fox

An All-Star Production. Released by Universal. Produced and directed by Chester Erskine. Screenplay by Chester Erskine. Based on the play by Paul and Claire Sifton. Running time, 80 minutes.

CAST

Stella Weldon	Sidney Fox
Edward Weldon	O. P. HEGGIE
Nolan	Henry HULL
Mrs. Weldon	Margaret Wycherly
Joe Biggers	Lynne Overman
Ada Biggers	Katherine Wilson
Arthur Weldon	Richard Whorf
Garboni	Humphrey Bogart
Henry McGrath	Granville Bates
Elizabeth McGrath	Cora Witherspoon
District Attorney Plunkett	Moffat Johnston
Ingersoll	Henry O'Neill
Ethel Saxon	Helen Flint

SYNOPSIS

Ethel Saxon, on trial for murdering the man who betrayed her, is convicted after Edward Weldon, foreman of the jury, asks her, "Did you take his money after you killed him?" and she answers, "Yes." Held responsible for sentencing the woman to death, Weldon is persecuted by the press, but he insists he would do the same thing again if necessary, even though someone he loved were involved. That opportunity unexpectedly comes to him.

Weldon's daughter, Stella, believes herself in love with Garboni, a gangster. Forced to flee from the police, Garboni tells her they are through. At midnight, as Ethel Saxon is going to the electric chair, Stella meets Garboni in his car and kills him with his own gun. She returns home and confesses.

The District Attorney, who has benefited from the Saxon trial publicity, frames a far-fetched theory that Stella did not kill Garboni at all, but merely was suffering from the delusions of an over-imaginative mind. He convinces Weldon that there is no need to prosecute and that Weldon is not violating the law in shielding Stella from the police.

With Sidney Fox, Henry Hull, and Lynne Overman

The Petrified Forest
1936

A Warner Bros. Picture. Directed by Archie Mayo. Associate producer, Henry Blanke. Screenplay by Charles Kenyon and Delmer Daves. Based on the play by Robert E. Sherwood. Director of photography, Sol Polito. Music by Bernhard Kaun. Film editor, Owen Marks. Assistant director, Dick Mayberry. Art director, John Hughes. Gowns by Orry-Kelly. Special effects by Warren E. Lynch, Fred Jackman and Willard Van Enger. Sound recorder, Charles Lang. Running time, 83 minutes.

CAST

Alan Squier	LESLIE HOWARD
Gabrielle Maple	BETTE DAVIS
Mrs. Chisholm	Genevieve Tobin
Boze Hertzlinger	Dick Foran
Duke Mantee	Humphrey Bogart
Jackie	Joseph Sawyer
Jason Maple	Porter Hall
Gramp Maple	Charley Grapewin
Mr. Chisholm	Paul Harvey
Lineman	Eddie Acuff
Ruby	Adrian Morris
Paula	Nina Campana
Slim	Slim Thompson
Joseph	John Alexander

SYNOPSIS

Alan Squier, a poet-intellectual wandering across the country, comes to a desert gas station–café in Arizona's Petrified Forest. He makes friends with the waitress,

With Bette Davis and Leslie Howard

Gabrielle Maple, who shares his artistic aspirations and love of poetry. The two find in each other quick sympathy and understanding, arousing the jealousy of Boze, the station attendant and Gabrielle's suitor. Alan, however, is intent on continuing his journey and accepts a ride with the Chisholms, a couple who have stopped for gas.

With Charley Grapewin, Genevieve Tobin, Leslie Howard, Paul Harvey, Bette Davis, Slim Thompson, and Joseph Sawyer

With Leslie Howard and Bette Davis

On the road they are stopped by Duke Mantee, a notorious killer who has escaped from prison. Commandeering the Chisholm's car, Mantee and his three henchmen drive off, leaving the occupants afoot. Alan and the Chisholms make their way back to the café, only to find Mantee there, holding Gabrielle, her grandfather, and Boze prisoners. Mantee plans a getaway across the Mexican border, but is waiting for his girl friend to arrive in another car.

At the mercy of Mantee, Alan and Gabrielle's friendship ripens, he seeing in her a kindred artistic spirit with something of the promise he once felt was his. Gabrielle wants to go to France, her mother's birthplace, to study art, but Gramp Maple is holding on to his money. Making over his life insurance—his only worldly pos-

session—to Gabrielle, Alan proposes that Mantee kill him when he leaves, and the gangster amusedly consents.

The police, tracking Mantee, close in, and the gang prepares to escape. Alan reminds the Duke of his promise, and Mantee shoots him down. Content in the realization that he has enabled Gabrielle to carry on in the paths he had hoped to walk, Alan dies in her arms.

In this film both Howard and Bogart played the roles they created in the original Broadway play. In 1955, two decades after appearing in the stage version, Bogart portrayed "Duke Mantee" a third time in a television production of *The Petrified Forest*, with Henry Fonda as "Alan" and Lauren Bacall as "Gabrielle."

With Joseph Sawyer, Leslie Howard,
Genevieve Tobin, Paul Harvey,
John Alexander, and Adrian Morris

28

With Edward G. Robinson

With Barton MacLane

Bullets or Ballots

1936

A First National Picture for Warner Bros. Directed by William Keighley. Associate producer, Louis F. Edelman. Screenplay by Seton I. Miller. Based on an original story by Martin Mooney and Seton I. Miller. Director of photography, Hal Mohr. Music by Heinz Roemheld. Film editor, Jack Killifer. Assistant director, Chuck Hansen. Art director, Carl Jules Weyl. Special effects by Fred Jackman, Fred Jackman, Jr., and Warren E. Lynch. Sound recorder, Oliver S. Garretson. Running time, 81 minutes.

CAST

Johnny Blake	EDWARD G. ROBINSON
Lee Morgan	Joan BLONDELL
Al Kruger	Barton MacLANE
Nick "Bugs" Fenner	Humphrey BOGART
Herman	Frank McHUGH
Captain Dan McLaren	Joseph King
Driscoll	Richard Purcell
Wires	George E. Stone
Grand Jury Spokesman	Joseph Crehan
Bryant	Henry O'Neill
Hollister	Henry Kolker
Thorndyke	Gilbert Emery
Caldwell	Herbert Rawlinson
Nellie	Louise Beavers
Vinci	Norman Willis
Crail	William Pawley
Kelly	Ralph Remley
Gatley	Frank Faylen

With Frank McHugh
and Joan Blondell

SYNOPSIS

With a mob headed by Al Kruger in control, New York rackets flourish under a supine administration that has demoted tough cop Johnny Blake to an outlying precinct. Masterminding the mob is a triumvirate of bankers whose political, financial, and social influence permits the rackets to exist. When Bryant, a crusading editor, is murdered, a grand jury appoints Captain Dan McLaren to smash the rackets. McLaren ostensibly fires Blake from the police force, and Blake, bitter, joins the mob as Kruger's right-hand man. Nick Fenner, Kruger's lieutenant and Bryant's killer, is suspicious of Blake and resents the ex-cop's presence in the mob.

Blake, who in reality is cooperating with McLaren, reveals gangland plans to the police, who conduct a series of raids on the rackets' operations. To compensate for the mob's reduction in revenue, Blake proposes going into the numbers racket, heretofore run on a small scale by Blake's girl friend, Lee Morgan. Kruger adopts Blake's suggestion, and the mob's success is so great that Kruger neglects the other rackets. Angered, Fenner kills Kruger, and in the ensuing struggle for leadership Blake takes over and learns the identity of the three bankers.

When Fenner's produce racket is broken up by the police and a lookout spots Blake as the fingerman, Fenner goes to kill Blake. In a gun battle Fenner is killed and Blake mortally wounded, but Blake lives long enough to lead McLaren to the bankers, with whose arrest the rackets are broken.

With Garry Owen

With Joan Blondell

Two Against the World
1936

A First National Picture for Warner Bros. Directed by William McGann. Associate producer, Bryan Foy. Screenplay by Michel Jacoby. Based on the play Five Star Final *by Louis Weitzenkorn. Director of photography, Sid Hickox. Music by Heinz Roemheld. Film editor, Frank Magee. Dialogue director, Irving Rapper. Assistant director, Carrol Sax. Art director, Esdras Hartley. Special effects by Fred Jackman, Jr., and Rex Wimpy. Sound recorder, C. A. Riggs. Running time, 64 minutes.*

CAST

Sherry Scott	Humphrey BOGART
Alma Ross	Beverly ROBERTS
Martha Carstairs	Helen MacKellar
Jim Carstairs	Henry O'Neill
Edith Carstairs	Linda Perry
Billy Sims	Carlyle Moore, Jr.
Mrs. Marion Sims	Virginia Brissac
Bertram C. Reynolds	Robert Middlemass
Mr. Banning	Clay Clement
Martin Leavenworth	Harry Hayden
Cora Latimer	Claire Dodd
Tippy Mantus	Hobart Cavanaugh
Malcolm Sims	Douglas Wood
Herman O'Reilly	Bobby Gordon
Miss Symonds	Paula Stone
Tommy	Frank Orth
Dr. McGuire	Howard Hickman
Sound Mixer	Ferdinand Schumann-Heink

With Beverly Roberts

With Claire Dodd

With Harry Hayden and Linda Perry

SYNOPSIS

The unscrupulous owner of a radio station, sacrificing quality for more profitable sensationalism, broadcasts a serial based on a twenty-year-old murder case. Martha Carstairs, the woman charged with the crime, was exonerated by a jury and afterwards was happily married, but she has never spoken of the case to her daughter Edith, who is engaged to marry Billy Sims, son of a wealthy manufacturer.

The unnecessary revival of the sordid case causes Martha's identity to be discovered and made public,

jeopardizing Edith's wedding. Unable to bear the results of the revelation, Martha and her husband commit suicide.

The policy that leads to this tragedy is opposed by the station manager, Sherry Scott, who is encouraged in his stand by his secretary, Alma Ross. They are then "two against the world" until Edith accuses the broadcast executives of "murdering" her parents, and the radio commission, with Scott's help, steps in to clean up the station's programming.

With Linda Perry,
Carlyle Moore, Jr.,
Harry Hayden,
Robert Middlemass,
and Clay Clement

32

With Walter Miller, Ross Alexander,
and Carlyle Moore, Jr.

China Clipper
1936

*A First National Picture for Warner Bros. Directed by
Ray Enright. Associate producer, Louis F. Edelman.
Original screenplay by Frank Wead. Director of pho-
tography, Arthur Edeson. Music by Bernhard Kaun
and W. Franke Harling. Film editor, Owen Marks.
Dialogue director, Gene Lewis. Assistant director, Lee
Katz. Art director, Max Parker. Gowns by Orry-Kelly.
Aerial photography by Elmer G. Dyer and H. F. Koene-
kamp. Special effects by Fred Jackman, Willard Van
Enger, and H. F. Koenekamp. Sound recorder, Everett
A. Brown. Technical adviser, William I. Van Dusen,
Pan-American Airways. Running time, 85 minutes.*

CAST

Dave Logan	PAT O'BRIEN
Jean Logan	Beverly ROBERTS
Tom Collins	ROSS ALEXANDER
Hap Stuart	Humphrey BOGART
Sunny Avery	Marie WILSON
Dad Brunn	Henry B. Walthall
Jim Horn	Joseph Crehan
Mr. Pierson	Joseph King
B. C. Hill	Addison Richards
Mother Brunn	Ruth Robinson
Radio Operator	Carlyle Moore, Jr.
Co-Pilot	Lyle Moraine
Co-Pilot	Dennis Moore
Navigator	Wayne Morris
Bill Andrews	Alexander Cross
Pilot	William Wright
Commerce Inspector	Kenneth Harlan
Secretary	Anne Nagel
Secretary	Marjorie Weaver
Radio Operator	Milburn Stone
Radio Operator	Owen King

With Ross Alexander, Carlyle Moore, Jr.,
and Wayne Morris

With Pat O'Brien, Carlyle Moore, Jr.,
Lyle Moraine, Dennis Moore,
Wayne Morris and Ross Alexander

With Pat O'Brien, Henry B. Walthall,
and Ross Alexander

SYNOPSIS

Dave Logan, inspired by Lindbergh's conquest of the Atlantic, plans a trans-Pacific airline. With flying buddy Tom Collins, designer Dad Brunn, and backer B. C. Hill, Logan starts a Washington-Philadelphia line, but it succumbs to financial troubles. Still pursuing his dream, Logan, joined by ace flyer Hap Stuart, prevails upon Collins and Brunn to experiment with him on the first clipper ships to fly the Caribbean. The success of this line intensifies Logan's desire to span the Pacific.

His selfish devotion to his ambition causes his wife, Jean, to leave him, Stuart to desert him, and Dad Brunn to work himself to death on plans for the China Clipper. Logan mortgages his South American line to finance the Pacific flight, and his sacrifice brings Stuart back to him as pilot of the Clipper. Fighting time and the weather, the Clipper completes its successful flight to China. Logan's work is vindicated, but he is sobered by the cost of his success, and he and Jean are reunited.

With Dennis Moore, Ross Alexander,
Carlyle Moore, Jr., and Walter Miller

Isle of Fury
1936

A Warner Bros. Picture. Directed by Frank McDonald. Associate producer, Bryan Foy. Screenplay by Robert Andrews and William Jacobs. Based on the novel The Narrow Corner *by W. Somerset Maugham. Director of photography, Frank Good. Music by Howard Jackson. Film editor, Warren Low. Assistant director, Frank Heath. Art director, Esdras Hartley. Gowns by Orry-Kelly. Special effects by Fred Jackman, Willard Van Enger, and H. F. Koenekamp. Sound recorder, Charles Lang. Running time, 60 minutes.*

With Margaret Lindsay

With E. E. Clive, Donald Woods, and Margaret Lindsay

CAST

Val Stevens	Humphrey BOGART
Lucille Gordon	Margaret LINDSAY
Eric Blake	Donald WOODS
Captain Deever	Paul Graetz
Anderson	Gordon Hart
Dr. Hardy	E. E. Clive
Otar	George Regas
Sam	Sidney Bracy
Kim Lee	Tetsu Komai
Oh Kay	Miki Morita
The Rector	Houseley Stevenson, Sr.
Old Native	Frank Lackteen

With Donald Woods and Margaret Lindsay

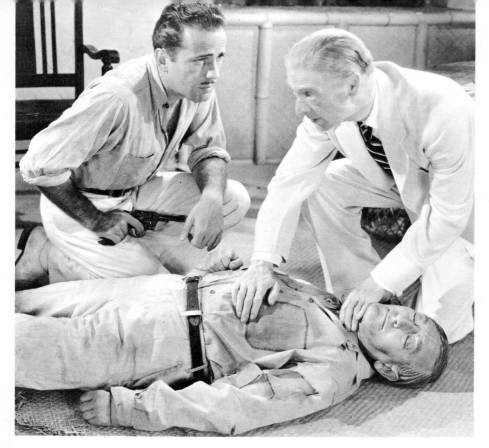

With E. E. Clive

SYNOPSIS

On an island in the South Seas, Val Stevens and Lucille Gordon are being married. As the ceremony concludes, word is brought that a ship is going down on an offshore reef. Val rescues Captain Deever and a passenger, Eric Blake. Eric accompanies Val and his wife on a pearl-fishing expedition and saves Val from an octopus. A friendship grows between the two men.

An incipient love affair between Eric and Lucille is arrested by Dr. Hardy, who slyly lectures Eric over highballs. Hardy, believing that Eric is wanted in the States, tells Val of the romance. When Val confronts the pair, it is revealed that Val himself is the fugitive and that Eric is the detective sent to get him. Seeing that Val is living a reformed life with Lucille, Eric calls the case closed and leaves the island.

With Donald Woods
and E. E. Clive

36

With Erin O'Brien-Moore

With Erin O'Brien-Moore

Black Legion
1937

A Warner Bros. Picture. Directed by Archie Mayo. Associate producer, Robert Lord. Screenplay by Abem Finkel and William Wister Haines. Based on an original story by Robert Lord. Director of photography, George Barnes. Music by Bernhard Kaun. Film editor, Owen Marks. Assistant director, Jack Sullivan. Art director, Robert Haas. Gowns by Milo Anderson. Special effects by Fred Jackman, Jr., and H. F. Koenekamp. Sound recorder, C. A. Riggs. Running time, 83 minutes.

With Joseph Sawyer

With Eddie Chandler and Robert Homans

With Helen Flint

38

Frank Taylor, a factory workman, becomes embittered when he loses a foremanship to a man who is foreign-born. He hears of the "pro-American" Black Legion, a secret organization patterned after the Ku Klux Klan. Joining the Legion in impressive initiation rites, Frank spends more and more time away from home participating in the hooded order's reign of terror. His wife's suspicions are aroused, but when she questions him he strikes her and she leaves him.

Ed Jackson, Frank's best friend, learns that the Legion is responsible for several recent atrocities when Frank divulges the secret while drunk. Panic-stricken at revealing Legion secrets to an outsider, Frank informs an officer of the clan. Ed is abducted by the Legion and taken into the woods to be flogged. When he tries to escape he is shot and killed by Frank himself.

Caught and accused of the slaying, Frank is contacted by racketeers who organized the pseudo-patriotic Legion for their own profit. They have prepared a story of self-defense for him to tell at the trial. Only when his testimony casts discredit on his wife does he balk and turn state's evidence, indicting the Legion and implicating several clan members attending the trial. Frank and the other clansmen are sentenced to life imprisonment.

With Erin O'Brien-Moore
and Ann Sheridan

With Dickie Jones

The Great O'Malley

1937

A Warner Bros. Picture. Directed by William Dieterle. Associate producer, Harry Joe Brown. Screenplay by Milton Krims and Tom Reed. Based on the story "The Making of O'Malley" by Gerald Beaumont. Director of photography, Ernest Haller. Music by Heinz Roemheld. Film editor, Warren Low. Dialogue director, Irving Rapper. Assistant director, Frank Shaw. Art director, Hugh Reticker. Gowns by Milo Anderson. Special effects by James Gibbons, Fred Jackman, Jr., and H. F. Koenekamp. Sound recorder, Francis J. Scheid. Orchestrations by Hugo Friedhofer. Running time, 71 minutes.

With Granville Bates

With Frieda Inescort,
Pat O'Brien, and Sybil Jason

With Pat O'Brien and Sybil Jason

CAST

James Aloysius O'Malley	PAT O'BRIEN
Barbara Phillips	SYBIL JASON
John Phillips	Humphrey BOGART
Judy Nolan	Ann SHERIDAN
Mrs. Phillips	Frieda INESCORT
Captain Cromwell	Donald Crisp
Defense Attorney	Henry O'Neill
Motorist	Craig Reynolds
Pinky Holden	Hobart Cavanaugh
Doctor	Gordon Hart
Mrs. O'Malley	Mary Gordon
Mrs. Flaherty	Mabel Colcord
Father Patrick	Frank Sheridan
Miss Taylor	Lillian Harmer
Tubby	Delmar Watson
Dr. Larson	Frank Reicher

SYNOPSIS

O'Malley, an overzealous officer with an eye for the letter of the law, makes himself despised by issuing citations for petty infractions. He arrests John Phillips for a minor traffic violation, causing him to lose a chance for a job. Desperate to provide for his wife and crippled child, Phillips commits a robbery, but is caught by O'Malley and sent to prison.

Given up as impossible by Captain Cromwell, O'Malley is relegated to traffic cop at a school crossing, where he becomes very fond of little Barbara Phillips. He also falls in love with Barbara's teacher, Judy Nolan, whose effective scorn tempers his martinet spirit. When he finds that Barbara is the daughter of the man he sent to jail, he provides for her and her mother, pays for an operation that corrects the child's lameness, and secretly helps arrange Phillips' parole.

Unaware of O'Malley's help and bent only on revenge, Phillips shoots the officer, but O'Malley, humanized by his experiences, claims the shooting was an accident, and Phillips is exonerated. O'Malley recovers and returns to his old beat, reinstated in the respect of the police force and in the affections of Judy.

With Bette Davis

With Bette Davis

Marked Woman
1937

A First National Picture for Warner Bros. Directed by Lloyd Bacon. Associate producer, Louis F. Edelman. Original screenplay by Robert Rossen and Abem Finkel. Director of photography, George Barnes. Music by Bernhard Kaun and Heinz Roemheld. Film editor, Jack Killifer. Assistant director, Dick Mayberry. Art director, Max Parker. Gowns by Orry-Kelly. Special effects by James Gibbons and Robert Burks. Sound recorder, Everett A. Brown. Songs: "My Silver Dollar Man" by Harry Warren and Al Dubin; "Mr. and Mrs. Doaks" by M. K. Jerome and Jack Scholl. Running time, 96 minutes.

With Henry O'Neill

CAST

Mary Dwight	BETTE DAVIS
David Graham	Humphrey BOGART
Gabby Marvin	Lola Lane
Emmy Lou Egan	Isabel Jewell
Johnny Vanning	Eduardo Cianelli
Florrie Liggett	Rosalind Marquis
Estelle Porter	Mayo Methot
Betty	Jane Bryan
Louie	Allen Jenkins
Gordon	John Litel
Charlie	Ben Welden
Ralph Krawford	Damian O'Flynn
Arthur Sheldon	Henry O'Neill
Lawyer at Jail	Raymond Hatton
Headwaiter	Carlos San Martin
Bob Crandall	William B. Davidson
Eddie	Kenneth Harlan
George Beler	Robert Strange
Bell Captain	James Robbins
John Truble	Arthur Aylesworth
Vincent	John Sheehan
Mac	Sam Wren
Detective Casey	Edwin Stanley
Henchman	Alan Davis
Henchman	Allen Mathews
Detective Ferguson	Guy Usher
Judge at First Trial	Gordon Hart
Judge at Second Trial	Pierre Watkin
Joe	Herman Marks

With Betty Davis, Mayo Methot, and Rosalind Marquis

SYNOPSIS

Vice czar Johnny Vanning takes control of a swank New York night club. His "hostesses"—Mary, Gabby, Emmy Lou, Florrie, and Estelle—are exploited and terrorized into submission. Mary lures a roistering guest into spending more than he has, and when he can't pay he is killed. District Attorney David Graham, thinking he has an open-and-shut case, brings Vanning to trial, but Mary, intimidated by Vanning, gives testimony that saves him. Mary's sister, Betty, goes to a party at Vanning's club against Mary's wishes and is accidentally killed by Vanning while resisting the advances of a Vanning henchman. When Mary threatens retaliation she is beaten and her face scarred, but she determines to expose Vanning. Mary and her friends turn state's evidence and tell their story to Graham, who convicts Vanning and breaks up his vice ring. As Graham is acclaimed a crusader, the five girls walk off together into the night.

With Ralph Dunn, Gordon Hart, and Bette Davis

With Harry Carey, William Haade and Edward G. Robinson

With William Haade and Ben Welden

Kid Galahad
1937

A Warner Bros. Picture. Directed by Michael Curtiz. Associate producer, Samuel Bischoff. Screenplay by Seton I. Miller. Based on the novel by Francis Wallace. Director of photography, Tony Gaudio. Music by Heinz Roemheld and Max Steiner. Film editor, George Amy. Dialogue director, Irving Rapper. Assistant director, Jack Sullivan. Art director, Carl Jules Weyl. Gowns by Orry-Kelly. Special effects by James Gibbons and Edwin B. DuPar. Sound recorder, Charles Lang. Orchestrations by Hugo Friedhofer. Song, "The Moon Is in Tears Tonight," by M. K. Jerome and Jack Scholl. Running time, 101 minutes.

CAST

Nick Donati	EDWARD G. ROBINSON
Fluff	BETTE DAVIS
Turkey Morgan	Humphrey BOGART
Ward Guisenberry	Wayne MORRIS
Marie Donati	Jane BRYAN
Silver Jackson	Harry CAREY
Chuck McGraw	William Haade
Mrs. Donati	Soledad Jiminez
Joe Taylor	Joe Cunningham
Buzz Barett	Ben Welden
Brady	Joseph Crehan
The Redhead	Veda Ann Borg
Barney	Frank Faylen
Gunman	Harland Tucker
Sam	Bob Evans
Burke	Hank Hankinson
O'Brien	Bob Nestell
Denbaugh	Jack Kranz
Referee	George Blake

With Harry Carey, Wayne Morris,
Edward G. Robinson, and
William Haade

Synopsis

Fight manager Nick Donati, dreaming of discovering a fighter he can develop into a champion, comes upon one accidentally when a bellhop named Ward Guisenberry knocks out champ Chuck McGraw in a hotel-room fracas. Christened "Kid Galahad" by Fluff, Nick's mistress, Ward is signed up and sent to Nick's farm to train, accompanied by Fluff and trainer Silver Jackson. Here the Kid meets Nick's young sister, Marie, and the two fall in love. When Nick finds the Kid romantically involved with his convent-sheltered sister, and Fluff herself yearning for the young fighter's affections, he vengefully arranges a bout with McGraw, thinking the Kid unprepared for a championship fight.

Meeting with Turkey Morgan, McGraw's gangster-manager, Nick guarantees that the Kid will lose and tells Morgan that he is betting against his own fighter. Knowing that McGraw can slug but can't box, Nick instructs Ward to slug, and for seven rounds the Kid takes a savage beating. Fluff and Marie plead with Nick to save the Kid until Nick finally relents and reverses his ring instructions. The Kid wins by a knock-out. Morgan, double-crossed, forces his way into the Kid's dressing room, and in an exchange of gunfire both Nick and Morgan are killed. Kid Galahad is acclaimed heavyweight champion of the world, a title he abdicates in favor of marrying Marie.

With William Haade and
Edward G. Robinson

With Pat O'Brien

With Ann Sheridan

With Ann Sheridan and Pat O'Brien

San Quentin
1937

A First National Picture for Warner Bros. Directed by Lloyd Bacon. Associate producer, Samuel Bischoff. Screenplay by Peter Milne and Humphrey Cobb. Based on an original story by Robert Tasker and John Bright. Director of photography, Sid Hickox. Music by Heinz Roemheld, Charles Maxwell, and David Raksin. Film editor, William Holmes. Assistant director, Dick Mayberry. Art director, Esdras Hartley. Gowns by Howard Shoup. Special effects by James Gibbons and H. F. Koenekamp. Sound recorder, Everett A. Brown. Orchestrations by Joseph Nussbaum and Ray Heindorf. Song, "How Could You?" by Harry Warren and Al Dubin. Running time, 70 minutes.

CAST

Capt. Stephen Jameson	PAT O'BRIEN
Joe "Red" Kennedy	HUMPHREY BOGART
May Kennedy	Ann SHERIDAN
Lieut. Druggin	Barton MacLANE
Sailor Boy Hansen	Joseph Sawyer
Helen	Veda Ann Borg
Mickey Callahan	James Robbins
Warden Taylor	Joseph King
Captain	Gordon Oliver
Dopey	Garry Owen
Venetti	Marc Lawrence
Lieutenant	Emmett Vogan
Convict	William Pawley
Convict	Al Hill
Prison Runner	Max Wagner
Convict	George Lloyd
Fink	Ernie Adams

SYNOPSIS

Steve Jameson, an ex-army officer, takes the job of yard captain at San Quentin prison. He falls in love with May, a café singer whose brother, Joe, is arrested for robbery and sentenced to San Quentin. Jameson institutes a merit system intended to separate unfortunate lawbreakers from habitual criminals, and Joe is assigned to a road camp as a step in his rehabilitation. Lieutenant Druggin, who resents Jameson's meth-

With Pat Flaherty, Ann Sheridan,
Edward Keane, and Pat O'Brien (right)

With Joseph Sawyer and
Barton MacLane

With Joseph Sawyer

ods, assigns Hansen, a hardened convict, to the camp
and plants suspicions in Joe's mind about Jameson's
relationship with May.

Aided by Helen, Hansen's moll, Joe and Hansen
escape from the road gang. Joe makes his way to May's
apartment, where Jameson has gone to trace the fleeing convict. Joe shoots Jameson, wounding him, but
Joe is disabused of his suspicions when May tells him
that she and Jameson are in love. Joe decides to return
to prison and give himself up, but on the way he is shot
by police. Mortally wounded, he staggers back to San
Quentin and dies at the prison gates, his last words a
plea for the convicts to cooperate with Jameson.

Dead End
1937

A Samuel Goldwyn Production. Released through United Artists. Directed by William Wyler. Produced by Samuel Goldwyn. Associate producer, Merritt Hulburd. Screenplay by Lillian Hellman. Based on the play by Sidney Kingsley. Director of photography, Gregg Toland. Film editor, Daniel Mandell. Dialogue director, Edward P. Goodnow. Assistant director, Eddie Bernoudy. Art director, Richard Day. Set decorations by Julia Heron. Costumes by Omar Kiam. Special effects by James Basevi. Sound recorder, Frank Maher. Musical director, Alfred Newman. Running time, 93 minutes.

With Allen Jenkins

CAST

Drina	SYLVIA SIDNEY
Dave Connell	JOEL MCCREA
Baby Face Martin	Humphrey BOGART
Kay Burton	Wendy BARRIE
Francey	Claire TREVOR
Hunk	Allen JENKINS
Mrs. Martin	Marjorie Main
Tommy	Billy Halop
Dippy	Huntz Hall
Angel	Bobby Jordan
Spit	Leo Gorcey
T. B.	Gabriel Dell
Milty	Bernard Punsley
Philip Griswold	Charles Peck
Mr. Griswold	Minor Watson
Officer Mulligan	James Burke
Doorman	Ward Bond
Mrs. Connell	Elisabeth Risdon
Mrs. Fenner	Esther Dale
Mr. Pascagli	George Humbert
Governess	Marcelle Corday
Whitey	Charles Halton

SYNOPSIS

The scene is a street on New York's East Side, terminating on the river front, where the fashionable apartments of the rich meet the tenement dwellings of the poor. Running riot are a gang of slum kids, respecting no law, their idols the gangsters, their ambition to live as their heroes do. Onto the street where he was raised comes Baby Face Martin, a notorious gangster, drawn back to his old haunts by a sentimental desire to see his mother and his childhood girl friend. He and his companion, Hunk, watch as the kids pursue another wasted day swimming in the river, heckling the doorman of a posh apartment house, tormenting Philip Griswold, a rich boy. Dave Connell, raised on

With Joel McCrea
and Allen Jenkins

With Allen Jenkins

With James Burke
and Joel McCrea

With Joel McCrea, Allen Jenkins,
and Charles Halton

the same street with Martin, recognizes him and warns him to stay away, but Martin contemptuously ignores him.

Dave, a frustrated architect who dreams of tearing down the slums, is swayed between the loves of Drina and of Kay. Drina is a shopgirl, striving for respectability, yearning to leave the slums, fighting to save her brother, Tommy, from becoming another Martin. Kay is the kept woman of a rich man; she loves Dave, but cannot face a life in the slums. The kids lure Philip into a cellar where they beat and rob him. When Mr. Griswold intervenes, Tommy stabs him in the arm and escapes.

Martin's visit is a disaster. His mother welcomes him

With Marjorie Main

With Allen Jenkins

with a slap and denounces him as a murderer. He finds that Francey, his boyhood sweetheart, is a common streetwalker. Bitter and disillusioned, he decides to salvage something from the day by kidnapping Philip. As he and Hunk make their plans with Whitey, an accomplice, Dave sees them and again warns Martin to leave. Martin knifes him and Hunk pushes him into the river, but he manages to pull himself from the water. Knocking out Hunk, Dave takes his gun and pursues the fleeing Martin, finally trapping him on a fire escape and killing him.

With Allen Jenkins and Claire Trevor

As a crowd gathers around Martin's body, the doorman recognizes Spit and identifies him to Officer Mulligan as one of the gang that attacked Philip. Spit informs on Tommy, who has returned to say goodbye to Drina before running away. Kay tells Dave she is going away with a man she does not love but who can offer her security. Tommy catches Spit and is about to knife him when Dave intervenes. He and Drina prevail upon Tommy to surrender to the police, and Dave offers his reward money to defend the boy. As Drina, Dave, and Tommy leave with Mulligan, the remaining kids saunter off into the night, singing "If I had the wings of an angel, over these prison walls I would fly."

With Marla Shelton and Leslie Howard

Stand-In
1937

A Walter Wanger Production. Released through United Artists. Directed by Tay Garnett. Produced by Walter Wanger. Screenplay by Gene Towne and Graham Baker. Based on the Saturday Evening Post *serial by Clarence Budington Kelland. Director of photography, Charles Clarke. Music by Heinz Roemheld. Film editors, Otho Lovering and Dorothy Spencer. Assistant director, Charles Kerr. Art director, Alexander Tuluboff; associate, Wade Rubottom. Costumes by Helen Taylor. Sound recorder, Paul Neal. Musical director, Rox Rommel. Running time, 90 minutes.*

With Marla Shelton and
Alan Mowbray

With Leslie Howard

CAST

Atterbury Dodd	LESLIE HOWARD
Lester Plum	JOAN BLONDELL
Douglas Quintain	Humphrey BOGART
Koslofski	Alan Mowbray
Thelma Cheri	Marla Shelton
Ivor Nassau	C. Henry Gordon
Potts	Jack Carson
Pennypacker, Sr.	Tully Marshall
Pennypacker, Jr.	J. C. Nugent
Pennypacker	William V. Mong

51

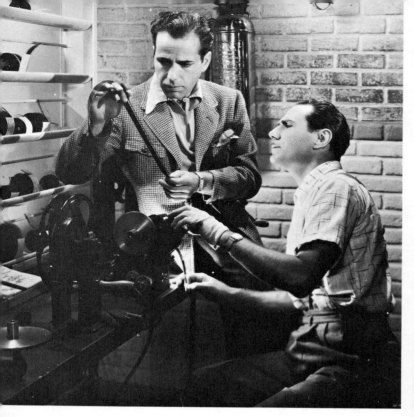

With Leslie Howard

With Marla Shelton

SYNOPSIS

Atterbury Dodd, bright young man of a New York banking house, is sent to Hollywood to determine whether Colossal Pictures should be continued in operation or sold as a bad investment. An efficiency expert, Dodd believes that all life and business can be reduced to a mathematical formula, but his ignorance of motion pictures is total. He is given a crash course in movie-making by Miss Lester Plum, stand-in for Colossal's ace star, Thelma Cheri. Cheri is making a jungle film called *Sex and Satan,* directed by a temperamental phoney named Koslofski. Doug Quintain, the producer, is romantically entangled with the petulant Cheri and has taken to drink.

Installing Miss Plum as his secretary, Dodd soon discovers that Cheri and Koslofski are conspiring with Nassau, a rival producer, to make Colossal's last-chance picture a flop. Dodd involves Cheri in a scandal, using it as an excuse to invalidate her contract, but his home office sells the studio out from under him, discharging all employees. Becoming a "stand-in" for Colossal's personnel and stockholders, Dodd persuades the employees to seize and hold the studio for forty-eight hours, while Quintain, weaned temporarily from the bottle, re-edits *Sex and Satan,* saving the picture by cutting out most of Cheri's scenes and making the gorilla the star.

Swing Your Lady

1938

A Warner Bros. Picture. Directed by Ray Enright. Associate producer, Samuel Bischoff. Screenplay by Joseph Schrank and Maurice Leo. Based on the play by Kenyon Nicholson and Charles Robinson. Director of photography, Arthur Edeson. Music by Adolph Deutsch. Film editor, Jack Killifer. Dialogue director, Jo Graham. Assistant director, Jesse Hibbs. Art director, Esdras Hartley. Gowns by Howard Shoup. Sound recorder, Charles Lang. Orchestrations by Hugo Friedhofer. Musical numbers created and directed by Bobby Connolly. Songs: "Mountain Swingaroo," "Hillbilly from Tenth Avenue," "The Old Apple Tree," "Swing Your Lady," and "Dig Me a Grave in Missouri" by M. K. Jerome and Jack Scholl. Running time, 79 minutes.

With Penny Singleton

CAST

Ed Hatch	Humphrey Bogart
Popeye Bronson	Frank McHugh
Sadie Horn	Louise Fazenda
Joe Skopapoulos	Nat Pendleton
Cookie Shannon	Penny Singleton
Shiner Ward	Allen Jenkins
Waldo Davis	Leon Weaver
Ollie Davis	Frank Weaver
Mrs. Davis	Elviry Weaver
Jack Miller	Ronald Reagan
Noah Webster	Daniel Boone Savage
Smith	Hugh O'Connell
Rufe Horn	Tommy Bupp
Len Horn	Sonny Bupp
Mattie Horn	Joan Howard
Mabel	Sue Moore
Hotel Proprietor	Olin Howland
Specialty Number	Sammy White

With Nat Pendleton, the Weaver Brothers, Penny Singleton, and Louis Fazenda

With Frank McHugh, Nat Pendleton, and Penny Singleton

SYNOPSIS

Barnstorming promoter Ed Hatch arrives in the Ozarks with his dimwitted wrestler, Joe Skopapoulos. Business is bad until Ed arranges a wrestling match between Joe and Sadie Horn, a mountaineer Amazon who plies the blacksmithing trade. But after a few rehearsal hammerlocks with the mighty widow, Joe's admiration is inflamed and he falls into dumb love. He goes on strike and refuses to wrestle.

When Noah, Sadie's jealous hillbilly suitor, shows up, Ed sees a chance to reactivate Joe by arranging a grudge bout, the winner to have Sadie as his bride. Joe vanquishes Noah, marries the lady blacksmith, and gives up the ring for horseshoeing.

Crime School
1938

A First National Picture for Warner Bros. Directed by Lewis Seiler. Associate producer, Bryan Foy. Screenplay by Crane Wilbur and Vincent Sherman. Based on an original story by Crane Wilbur. Director of photography, Arthur Todd. Music by Max Steiner. Film editor, Terry Morse. Dialogue director, Vincent Sherman. Assistant director, Fred Tyler. Art director, Charles Novi. Gowns by N'Was McKenzie. Sound recorder, Francis J. Scheid. Orchestrations by Hugo Friedhofer and George Parrish. Running time, 86 minutes.

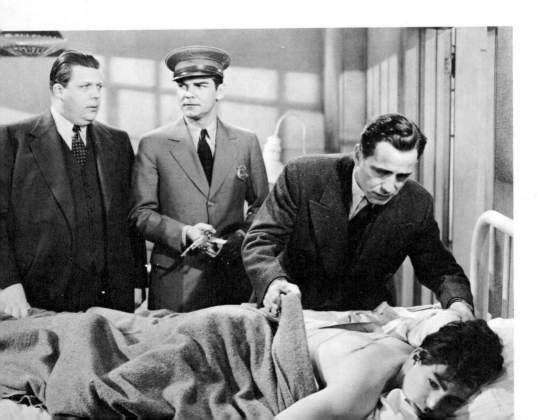

With Cy Kendall, Weldon Heyburn, and Billy Halop

CAST

Mark Braden	HUMPHREY BOGART
Sue Warren	Gale PAGE
Frankie Warren	Billy Halop
Squirt	Bobby Jordan
Goofy	Huntz Hall
Spike Hawkins	Leo Gorcey
Fats Papadopolo	Bernard Punsley
Bugs Burke	Gabriel Dell
Red	George Offerman, Jr.
Cooper	Weldon Heyburn
Morgan	Cy Kendall
Judge Clinton	Charles Trowbridge
Old Doctor	Spencer Charters
New Doctor	Donald Briggs
Commissioner	Frank Jaquet
Mrs. Burke	Helen MacKellar
Mr. Burke	Al Bridge
Mrs. Hawkins	Sibyl Harris
Nick Papadopolo	Paul Porcasi
Junkie	Frank Otto
Officer Hogan	Ed Gargan
Schwartz	James B. Carson

With Weldon Heyburn and Cy Kendall

SYNOPSIS

Six young hoodlums, sentenced to a reform school after one of them nearly kills a fence, encounter the brutal discipline of Morgan, the reformatory superintendent, who flogs their leader, Frankie, for attempting escape. On an inspection trip, Mark Braden, Deputy Commissioner of Correction, finds Frankie, untreated, in the hospital ward and the doctor drunk. Firing Morgan and the doctor, Braden assumes charge of the reformatory himself, winning the boys' cooperation by considerate treatment. Braden also falls in love with Frankie's sister, Sue.

Cooper, Morgan's aide, learns that Braden has discovered their embezzlement of school funds, and the two grafters plot to discredit Braden's methods by encouraging the boys to escape. Cooper falsely implies that Braden's consideration is due to Sue's acceptance of Braden's attentions. The boys escape in Cooper's car and go to Sue's apartment, but Braden and Sue dispel Frankie's suspicions, and Braden herds the boys back into their quarters before the Commissioner, alerted by Morgan, arrives for an inspection. Their scheme foiled and their graft uncovered, Morgan and Cooper are arrested. The boys are paroled in the custody of their parents.

With Billy Halop

With Weldon Heyburn, Cy Kendall, Frank Jaquet, John Ridgely (third from right), and others

Men Are Such Fools

1938

With Priscilla Lane

A Warner Bros. Picture. Directed by Busby Berkeley. Associate producer, David Lewis. Screenplay by Norman Reilly Raine and Horace Jackson. Based on the novel by Faith Baldwin. Director of photography, Sid Hickox. Music by Heinz Roemheld. Film editor, Jack Killifer. Dialogue director, Jo Graham. Assistant director, Chuck Hansen. Art director, Max Parker. Gowns by Howard Shoup. Sound recorder, Stanley Jones. Orchestrations by Ray Heindorf. Running time, 70 minutes.

CAST

Jimmy Hall	WAYNE MORRIS
Linda Lawrence	PRISCILLA LANE
Harry Galleon	Humphrey BOGART
Harvey Bates	Hugh Herbert
Nancy	Penny Singleton
Tad	Johnnie Davis
Beatrice Harris	Mona Barrie
Wanda Townsend	Marcia Ralston
Bill Dalton	Gene Lockhart
Mrs. Dalton	Kathleen Lockhart
George Onslow	Donald Briggs
Mrs. Pinkel	Renie Riano
Rudolf	Claude Allister
Mrs. Nelson	Nedda Harrigan
Mr. Nelson	Eric Stanley
Bill Collyer	James Nolan
June Cooper	Carole Landis

With Priscilla Lane

56

With Priscilla Lane

SYNOPSIS

Linda Lawrence skyrockets from a stenographer's desk to a job as account executive in an advertising agency. Though more interested in a career than in marriage, she falls in love with ex-football hero Jimmy Hall after his forceful courtship. They marry after Jimmy promises that he will not ask Linda to resign her position. Linda is pursued by her boss, Harvey Bates, and by Harry Galleon, a big radio contact man who can further her career if she will be "nice" to him. Jimmy becomes jealous, and Linda steps down to become a suburban housewife just as her name is becoming famous in the advertising and radio worlds.

Deciding that Jimmy is unambitious and content in a futureless job, Linda secretly promotes a junior partnership for him in an expanding firm. He refuses the job and she walks out on him, returning to her career. Jimmy then accepts the partnership and becomes successful, crashing the newspaper chatter columns as a Broadway playboy. After waiting a year for Jimmy to get in touch with her, Linda announces a trip to Paris, ostensibly to get a divorce and marry Harry, who has converted his proposition to a proposal. This brings Jimmy on the run to stop her, which of course is what she wanted all along. Their reconciliation throws Harry into the arms of Beatrice Harris, a sardonic vamp whom he had cast aside years before.

With Mona Barrie

With Mona Barrie and Priscilla Lane

With Edward G. Robinson and Claire Trevor

With Edward G. Robinson and Maxie Rosenbloom

The Amazing Dr. Clitterhouse
1938

A First National Picture for Warner Bros. Directed by Anatole Litvak. Associate producer, Robert Lord. Screenplay by John Wexley and John Huston. Based on the play by Barré Lyndon. Director of photography, Tony Gaudio. Music by Max Steiner. Film editor, Warren Low. Dialogue director, Jo Graham. Assistant director, Jack Sullivan. Art director, Carl Jules Weyl. Wardrobe by Milo Anderson. Sound recorder, C. A. Riggs. Orchestrations by George Parrish. Technical adviser, Dr. Leo Schulman. Running time, 87 minutes.

CAST

Dr. Clitterhouse	EDWARD G. ROBINSON
Jo Keller	Claire TREVOR
Rocks Valentine	Humphrey BOGART
Okay	Allen Jenkins
Inspector Lane	Donald Crisp
Nurse Randolph	Gale Page
Judge	Henry O'Neill
Prosecuting Attorney	John Litel
Grant	Thurston Hall
Butch	Maxie Rosenbloom
Pal	Bert Hanlon
Rabbit	Curt Bois
Tug	Ward Bond
Popus	Vladimir Sokoloff
Candy	Billy Wayne
Lieutenant Johnson	Robert Homans
Foreman of the Jury	Irving Bacon

With Maxie Rosenbloom, Edward G. Robinson, and Claire Trevor

With Bert Hanlon

SYNOPSIS

Dr. Clitterhouse, writing a book on the physiological reactions of criminals and wanting first-hand knowledge, becomes a criminal himself, committing several jewel robberies. He contacts a fence, Jo Keller, and finds to his surprise that the fence is a girl, working with a gang of safecrackers headed by Rocks Valentine. Clitterhouse joins the gang and, during a succession of robberies, makes notes on the thieves' reactions under tension. During the robbery of a fur warehouse, Rocks, jealous of the doctor's intellect and the attentions paid him by Jo, locks Clitterhouse in a cold-storage vault, but the doctor is freed by Butch, Jo's loyal henchman.

Completing his research, Clitterhouse bids farewell to the gang, but he is followed to his office by Rocks, who threatens to expose him as a criminal unless he continues his partnership with Rocks in a scheme to rob the doctor's own wealthy friends. Clitterhouse realizes there must be a final chapter to his book—one on homicide. He gives Rocks a poisoned drink and studies his reactions as he dies. Apprehended, Clitterhouse goes on trial for murder but is acquitted when he states that he was sane during the murder. The jury decides that any man who insists he was sane after making insanity his defense *must* be insane.

With Edward G. Robinson, Curt Bois, Claire Trevor, Maxie Rosenbloom, and Vladimir Sokoloff

With Edward G. Robinson, Bert Hanlon, Ward Bond, Maxie Rosenbloom, Allen Jenkins, Vladimir Sokoloff, Curt Bois, and Claire Trevor

With Joseph Downing and Norman Willis

Racket Busters
1938

A Warner Bros. Picture. A Cosmopolitan Production. Directed by Lloyd Bacon. Associate producer, Samuel Bischoff. Original screenplay by Robert Rossen and Leonardo Bercovici. Director of photography, Arthur Edeson. Music by Adolph Deutsch. Film editor, James Gibbon. Assistant director, Dick Mayberry. Art director, Esdras Hartley. Gowns by Howard Shoup. Sound recorder, Robert B. Lee. Orchestrations by Hugo Friedhofer. Running time, 71 minutes.

With Don Rowan, Norman Willis, George Brent, and Joseph Downing

CAST

Pete Martin	Humphrey BOGART
Denny Jordan	George BRENT
Nora Jordan	Gloria DICKSON
Horse Wilson	Allen JENKINS
Thomas Allison	Walter ABEL
Governor	Henry O'NEILL
Gladys	Penny Singleton
Crane	Anthony Averill
Pop Wilson	Oscar O'Shea
Charlie Smith	Elliott Sullivan
Mrs. Smith	Fay Helm
Joe	Joseph Downing
Gus	Norman Willis
Kimball	Don Rowan

dan reluctantly complies. The other truckers swing into line, and Martin appears to have won control when the legislature empowers Allison to jail witnesses who refuse to testify. Jordan's oldest friend, Pop Wilson, is murdered after testifying against Martin's henchmen, and Horse Wilson, Jordan's partner, ostracizes him and leaves trucking to become a commission merchant.

In a move to control the entire food market, Martin calls the truckers out on strike until every commission merchant and produce dealer joins his association. Horse attempts to rally the truckers against Martin and is shot by Martin's gunmen. Jordan leads the truckers in breaking the strike, and the truckers and the racketeers meet in a free-for-all. Jordan downs Martin in a hand-to-hand encounter as the police arrive.

With George Brent and Gloria Dickson

With George Brent (right)

SYNOPSIS

Pete Martin, Manhattan's most powerful gang chief, muscles in on the trucking business, the first step in his plan to control the entire produce market. Thomas Allison, appointed Special Prosecutor to smash the rackets, is confronted by a series of intimidated witnesses. Denny Jordan, popular and influential trucker and a loner, refuses to join Martin's organization, and his truck is burned.

To provide for his pregnant wife, Nora, Jordan robs the gang's office but is caught. Martin agrees to let him off if he will join the "protective association," and Jor-

61

With James Cagney

With James Cagney
and George Bancroft

Angels With Dirty Faces
1938

A First National Picture for Warner Bros. Directed by Michael Curtiz. Associate producer, Samuel Bischoff. Screenplay by John Wexley and Warren Duff. Based on an original story by Rowland Brown. Director of photography, Sol Polito. Music by Max Steiner. Film editor, Owen Marks. Dialogue director, Jo Graham. Assistant director, Sherry Shourds. Art director, Robert Haas. Gowns by Orry-Kelly. Sound recorder, Everett A. Brown. Orchestrations by Hugo Friedhofer. Technical adviser, Father J. J. Devlin. Running time, 97 minutes.

With James Cagney

gangster heroes. Rocky becomes the idol of the kids, teaching them crime and yet, at Connolly's request, forcing them to attend the parish play center.

Rocky contacts his lawyer, James Frazier, who has been holding $100,000 for him while he was in prison. Frazier is now prosperous in a night-club business, in partnership with Mac Keefer, a crooked politician. They refuse to give Rocky his money and his share in the business and attempt to have him killed, but Rocky escapes, kidnaps Frazier, and takes his money and incriminating papers. The three racketeers work together in an uncomfortable alliance until Father Connolly starts a radio and newspaper campaign to rid the community of crime rule. Frazier and Keefer decide to have Connolly murdered, but Rocky overhears their plan and kills them.

Sentenced to death, Rocky is visited in prison by Father Connolly, who tells him that the kids who worship him will become criminals like him if he goes to his death unbroken. At Connolly's request Rocky feigns cowardice in the electric chair. The kids refuse to believe newspaper accounts of Rocky's death until Father Connolly assures them that "he died like they said" and asks them to join him in saying a prayer "for a boy who couldn't run as fast as I could."

CAST

Rocky Sullivan	JAMES CAGNEY
Jerry Connolly	PAT O'BRIEN
James Frazier	Humphrey BOGART
Laury Ferguson	Ann SHERIDAN
Mac Keefer	George BANCROFT
Soapy	Billy Halop
Swing	Bobby Jordan
Bim	Leo Gorcey
Pasty	Gabriel Dell
Crab	Huntz Hall
Hunky	Bernard Punsley
Steve	Joseph Downing
Edwards	Edward Pawley
Blackie	Adrian Morris
Rocky as a boy	Frankie Burke
Jerry as a boy	William Tracy
Laury as a child	Marilyn Knowlden

St. Brendan's Church Choir

SYNOPSIS

Rocky Sullivan and Jerry Connolly, two tough East Side boys, are spotted by detectives breaking into a boxcar. The boys run and Jerry gets away, but Rocky is caught and sent to a reformatory. In the succeeding years Rocky becomes a Page One criminal, while Jerry becomes a priest assigned to their boyhood parish.

When Rocky finishes his latest stretch he returns to the old neighborhood and rents a room in a boarding-house run by Larry Ferguson, a former childhood playmate. He looks up Father Connolly, finds him attempting to retrieve a gang of slum kids from emulating their

Pat O'Brien

With John Eldredge

King of the Underworld
1939

A Warner Bros. Picture. Directed by Lewis Seiler. Associate producer, Bryan Foy. Screenplay by George Bricker and Vincent Sherman. Based on the Liberty Magazine serial Dr. Socrates by W. R. Burnett. Director of photography, Sid Hickox. Music by Heinz Roemheld. Film editor, Frank Dewar. Dialogue director, Vincent Sherman. Assistant director, Frank Heath. Art director, Charles Novi. Gowns by Orry-Kelly. Sound recorder, Everett A. Brown. Technical adviser, Dr. Leo Schulman. Running time, 69 minutes.

CAST

Joe Gurney	HUMPHREY BOGART
Carol Nelson	KAY FRANCIS
Bill Forrest	James Stephenson
Niles Nelson	John Eldredge
Aunt Margaret	Jessie Busley
Dr. Sanders	Arthur Aylesworth
Sheriff	Raymond Brown
Mr. Ames	Harland Tucker
Mr. Robert	Ralph Remley
Eddie	Charley Foy
Butch	Murray Alper
Porky	Joe Devlin
Mugsy	Elliott Sullivan
Slick	Alan Davis
Slats	John Harmon
Jerry	John Ridgely
Interne	Richard Bond
District Attorney	Pierre Watkin
Dr. Ryan	Charles Trowbridge
Dr. Jacobs	Edwin Stanley

With Kay Francis and James Stephenson

With Elliott Sullivan and James Stephenson

With Elliott Sullivan, Charley Foy,
Kay Francis, and James Stephenson

SYNOPSIS

Niles and Carol Nelson, partners in marriage and in medicine, save the life of a wounded henchman of underworld lord Joe Gurney. Learning of Niles' losses with bookmakers, Gurney encourages his weakness with gifts of money, placing Niles under virtual bondage to the gang. When another Gurney henchman is shot, Niles is forced to go to his aid, and Carol follows him. The gang's hideout is raided by the police, and Gurney, suspecting Niles of squealing, kills him. The gang escapes, and Carol faces trial as the fugitives' accomplice.

The fleeing Gurney, who has delusions of Napoleonic greatness, kidnaps Bill Forrest, a hitchhiking writer, and forces him to write his biography. When two of the mob are captured and imprisoned in a small town,

Carol establishes her medical practice there, hoping to prove her innocence at the trial. Gurney frees the two prisoners, but he is wounded during the jailbreak and goes to Carol to enlist her aid.

Making friends with Bill, who knows he will be killed when his writing job is finished, Carol plans the capture of the gang. She arranges for the police to close in. Meanwhile, she deliberately infects Gurney's wound. When he complains that his eyes are bothering him, Carol temporarily blinds the mobsters with an eyedrop solution under the pretext of saving them from infection. The blinded Gurney pursues Carol and Bill through the rooms of the hideout, trying to kill them, but the police arrive, shoot Gurney down, and rescue Carol and Bill.

With Kay Francis and
Charley Foy

The Oklahoma Kid
1939

A Warner Bros. Picture. Directed by Lloyd Bacon. Associate producer, Samuel Bischoff. Screenplay by Warren Duff, Robert Buckner and Edward E. Paramore. Based on an original story by Edward E. Paramore and Wally Klein. Director of photography, James Wong Howe. Music by Max Steiner. Film editor, Owen Marks. Assistant director, Dick Mayberry. Art director, Esdras Hartley. Gowns by Orry-Kelly. Sound recorder, Stanley Jones. Orchestrations by Hugo Friedhofer, Adolph Deutsch, George Parrish, and Murray Cutter. Technical adviser, Al Jennings. Running time, 80 minutes.

With Edward Pawley, Hugh Sothern, and Harvey Stephens

With Ward Bond

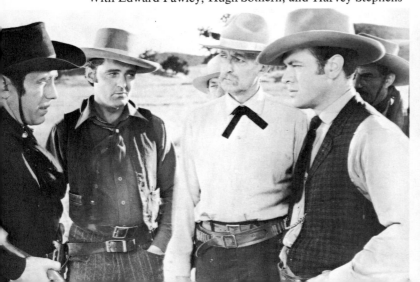

With James Cagney

With James Cagney

CAST

Jim Kincaid	JAMES CAGNEY
Whip McCord	Humphrey BOGART
Jane Hardwick	Rosemary LANE
Judge Hardwick	Donald CRISP
Ned Kincaid	Harvey STEPHENS
John Kincaid	Hugh Sothern
Alec Martin	Charles Middleton
Doolin	Edward Pawley
Wes Handley	Ward Bond
Curley	Lew Harvey
Indian Jack Pasco	Trevor Bardette
Ringo	John Miljan
Judge Morgan	Arthur Aylesworth
Hotel Clerk	Irving Bacon
Keely	Joe Devlin
Sheriff Abe Collins	Wade Boteler

SYNOPSIS

Jim Kincaid, black-sheep son of John Kincaid, is a notorious outlaw known as "The Oklahoma Kid." The Government, about to open the Cherokee Strip to settlers, has paid the Indians for their land, but the stage carrying the money is robbed by Whip McCord and his gang. The Kid ambushes the gang and makes off with the money. At a settlers' dance, the Kid meets Jane Hardwick, daughter of Judge Hardwick, and they are attracted to each other.

Before the new territory is opened McCord stakes a

67

"sooner" claim, and when John Kincaid and his son, Ned, arrive, they are forced to grant McCord the gambling and saloon concessions in exchange for the site they plan to develop into a town. Hoping to bring law and order to the area, Judge Hardwick and Ned campaign to elect Kincaid mayor, but when an opposition member is killed, McCord frames Kincaid and has him arrested for murder. Learning that the Kid is Kincaid's son, McCord incites a mob, led by three of his own men, to break into the jail and lynch the outlaw's father before his trial comes up.

Vowing vengeance, the Kid tracks down each of his father's murderers, killing two of them and bringing the third, Doolin, back to testify against McCord. The Kid and Ned find McCord in his saloon, but when Ned attempts to arrest him McCord shoots him. The Kid and McCord fight, and the Kid is nearly killed before his mortally wounded brother shoots McCord down. The Kid gives up his lawless ways and settles down with Jane.

With Trevor Bardette, Ward Bond, Ray Mayer, and James Cagney

With Bette Davis

With Bette Davis

Dark Victory
1939

A First National Picture for Warner Bros. Directed by Edmund Goulding. Associate producer, David Lewis. Screenplay by Casey Robinson. Based on the play by George Emerson Brewer, Jr., and Bertram Bloch. Director of photography, Ernest Haller. Music by Max Steiner. Film editor, William Holmes. Assistant director, Frank Heath. Art director, Robert Haas. Gowns by Orry-Kelly. Sound recorder, Robert B. Lee. Orchestrations by Hugo Friedhofer. Song, "Oh, Give Me Time for Tenderness," by Elsie Janis and Edmund Goulding. Technical adviser, Dr. Leo Schulman. Running time, 106 minutes.

CAST

Judith Traherne	BETTE DAVIS
Dr. Frederick Steele	George BRENT
Michael O'Leary	Humphrey BOGART
Ann King	Geraldine FITZGERALD
Alec Hamm	Ronald Reagan
Dr. Parsons	Henry Travers
Carrie Spottswood	Cora Witherspoon
Miss Wainwright	Dorothy Peterson
Martha	Virginia Brissac
Colonel Mantle	Charles Richman
Dr. Carter	Herbert Rawlinson
Dr. Driscoll	Leonard Mudie
Miss Dodd	Fay Helm
Lucy	Lottie Williams

With Cora Witherspoon, Geraldine Fitzgerald, Ronald Reagan, Bette Davis, and Charles Richman

With Bette Davis

SYNOPSIS

Judith Traherne, a fast-living young heiress, is troubled with increasingly frequent dizzy spells. Dr. Parsons refers her to Frederick Steele, a brain specialist, who finds her afflicted with a brain tumor and advises immediate surgery. The operation is successful and Judith falls in love with Steele, accepting his proposal of marriage.

Steele confides to Ann King, Judith's friend and secretary, that Judith's tumor in malignant and will prove fatal within ten months. Although both are anxious that she not know, Judith discovers the truth accidentally and thinks that Steele is marrying her out of pity. She returns to her carefree life with a vengeance, her only serious concern being her thoroughbred horse, Challenger, whom she hopes to enter in the Grand National. She is brought back to sanity by her Irish trainer, Michael O'Leary, who has himself been in love with her for many years. He points to her false

pride and urges her to enjoy what happiness she can while there is still time. Realizing he is right, Judith marries Steele and goes to live with him on his Vermont farm.

Steele, now retired from practice, devotes himself to research, hoping to find a cure for brain diseases such as Judith's. The months pass, and Judith's life is one of idyllic happiness. Michael comes with the news that he has entered Challenger in the Grand National, and Ann arrives for a visit. Then Judith's eyesight begins to fail, and she recognizes it as a symptom of approaching death. Steele is called away to a medical conference, and Judith sends him off without revealing that she knows the end is near. Ann helps her to her bedroom, where she lies waiting for the end to come, filled with the knowledge that her happiness and her courage have been a victory—though a dark victory—over death.

With Bette Davis and
Geraldine Fitzgerald

70

With Billy Halop

With Billy Halop and Harold Huber

You Can't Get Away With Murder
1939

A First National Picture for Warner Bros. Directed by Lewis Seiler. Associate producer, Samuel Bischoff. Screenplay by Robert Buckner, Don Ryan, and Kenneth Gamet. Based on the play Chalked Out *by Warden Lewis E. Lawes and Jonathan Finn. Director of photography, Sol Polito. Music by Heinz Roemheld. Film editor, James Gibbon. Dialogue director, Jo Graham. Assistant director, William Kissel. Art director, Hugh Reticker. Gowns by Milo Anderson. Sound recorder, Francis J. Scheid. Orchestrations by Hugo Friedhofer, Arthur Kay, and Rudolph Kopp. Running time, 78 minutes.*

CAST

Frank Wilson	HUMPHREY BOGART
Johnnie Stone	BILLY HALOP
Madge Stone	Gale PAGE
Attorney Carey	John Litel
Pop	Henry Travers
Fred Burke	Harvey Stephens
Scappa	Harold Huber
Red	Joseph Sawyer
Smitty	Joseph Downing
Toad	George E. Stone
Principal Keeper	Joseph King
Warden	Joseph Crehan
Gas Station Attendant	John Ridgely
District Attorney	Herbert Rawlinson

With Joseph Crehan, Billy Halop, and Joseph King

71

With Harvey Stephens,
Billy Halop, and
Frankie Burke

SYNOPSIS

Johnnie Stone embarks on a career of crime under the tutelage of Frank Wilson, a petty crook. First they steal a car and later hold up a gas station. They rob a pawnshop, and Wilson kills the pawnbroker with a gun stolen by Johnnie from his sister Madge's fiance, Fred Burke. Circumstantial evidence sends Burke to Sing Sing's death house, and Johnnie, terrorized by Wilson, remains silent.

Subsequently, Wilson and Johnnie are arrested for the car theft and also sent to Sing Sing. Here Wilson uses every wile and threat to keep Johnnie from breaking, but the boy begins to weaken under his sister's pleas and a cross-examination by Burke's lawyer, Carey. Wilson stages a prison break and takes Johnnie with him, expecting a chance to kill the boy during the confusion. The escape plot fails, and guards trap the pair in a boxcar. Wilson shoots Johnnie, but the boy makes a dying confession that removes Burke from the shadow of the electric chair and places Wilson there.

With Gale Page,
Billy Halop (Unidentified),
and Emory Parnell

The Roaring Twenties

1939

A Warner Bros.–First National Picture. Directed by Raoul Walsh. Executive producer, Hal B. Wallis. Associate producer, Samuel Bischoff. Screenplay by Jerry Wald, Richard Macaulay, and Robert Rossen. Based on an original story by Mark Hellinger. Director of photography, Ernest Haller. Music by Heinz Roemheld and Ray Heindorf. Film editor, Jack Killifer. Dialogue director, Hugh Cummings. Assistant director, Dick Mayberry. Art director, Max Parker. Wardrobe by Milo Anderson. Makeup artist, Perc Westmore. Special effects by Byron Haskin and Edwin B. DuPar. Sound recorder, Everett A. Brown. Songs: "My Melancholy Baby" by Ernie Burnett and George A. Norton; "I'm Just Wild About Harry" by Eubie Blake and Noble Sissle; "It Had to Be You" by Isham Jones and Gus Kahn; "In a Shanty in Old Shanty Town" by Jack Little, Joseph Young, and John Siras. Orchestral arrangements by Ray Heindorf. Narrated by John Deering. Running time, 106 minutes.

CAST

Eddie Bartlett	JAMES CAGNEY
Jean Sherman	PRISCILLA LANE
George Hally	Humphrey BOGART
Panama Smith	Gladys GEORGE
Lloyd Hart	Jeffrey LYNN
Danny Green	Frank McHUGH
Nick Brown	Paul KELLY
Mrs. Sherman	Elisabeth Risdon
Pete Henderson	Edward Keane
Sergeant Pete Jones	Joseph Sawyer
Mr. Fletcher	Joseph Crehan
Masters	George Meeker
Judge	John Hamilton
First Detective	Robert Elliott
Second Detective	Eddie Chandler
Lefty	Abner Biberman
Mrs. Gray	Vera Lewis
Eddie's Cellmate	Elliott Sullivan
Piano Accompanist	Bert Hanlon
First Mechanic	Murray Alper
Second Mechanic	Dick Wessel
Restaurant Proprietor	George Humbert
Tavern Proprietor	Ben Welden

With James Cagney and Jeffrey Lynn

With James Cagney and Frank McHugh

With James Cagney

nizes the watchman as his former sergeant and kills him. Learning of the killing, Lloyd quits the racket despite threats from George. As the rackets prosper, gang warfare increases, and Eddie sends Danny to arrange a truce between his mob and Brown's, but Brown sends Danny back dead. Eddie plans a reprisal, but George, resentful of Eddie's increasing power, tips off Brown, who sets a trap. Eddie kills Brown and escapes, but he no longer can trust George and dissolves their partnership.

Eddie, in love with Jean and blind to her romance with Lloyd, is astounded when Jean announces her intention to marry Lloyd. Eddie begins speculating in the stock market but loses everything in the 1929 crash. He sells his fleet of cabs to George, who mockingly leaves him one to drive himself. One day Eddie meets Jean in his cab and learns that Lloyd, now in the District Attorney's office, has received a death threat from George unless Lloyd stops preparing a case against him. Jean appeals to Eddie for help, and Eddie goes to George, urging him to lay off. When George refuses, Eddie kills him. Attempting to shoot his way past George's gunmen, Eddie is mortally wounded and dies on the steps of a nearby church.

SYNOPSIS

Three American soldiers in France during World War I part company after the Armistice. Lloyd Hart returns to a precarious law practice. George Hally, a former saloon keeper, becomes a bootlegger with the advent of Prohibition. Eddie Bartlett, a garage mechanic, finds his old job filled and, at the suggestion of his friend Danny Green, takes a job driving a cab. When Eddie is arrested for delivering a package of liquor to Panama Smith, Panama pays his fine, and they go into the bootleg liquor business together. Eddie builds up a fleet of cabs, using them to make his liquor deliveries, and when legal complications arise, he hires Lloyd as his lawyer. Jean Sherman, Eddie's wartime correspondence sweetheart, gets a job through Eddie singing in Henderson's cabaret, where Panama is hostess. Eddie introduces Lloyd to Jean, and they fall in love.

When bootlegger Nick Brown refuses to deal with him, Eddie hijacks a shipload of Brown's liquor, finds the shipment charged to George Hally, now Brown's aide. George proposes that he and Eddie become partners, and Eddie agrees. They tip off the Feds that Brown is running a liquor shipment, then raid the warehouse where the confiscated liquor is stored. George recog-

With Jeffrey Lynn and James Cagney

With Al Hill and James Cagney

The Return of Doctor X

1939

A First National Picture for Warner Bros. Directed by Vincent Sherman. Associate producer, Bryan Foy. Screenplay by Lee Katz. Based on the story "The Doctor's Secret" by William J. Makin. Director of photography, Sid Hickox. Music by Bernhard Kaun. Film editor, Thomas Pratt. Dialogue director, John Langan. Assistant director, Dick Mayberry. Art director, Esdras Hartley. Gowns by Milo Anderson. Makeup artist, Perc Westmore. Sound recorder, Charles Lang. Technical adviser, Dr. Leo Schulman. Running time, 62 minutes.

CAST

Walter Barnett	WAYNE MORRIS
Joan Vance	ROSEMARY LANE
Marshall Quesne	HUMPHREY BOGART
Michael Rhodes	Dennis MORGAN
Dr. Francis Flegg	John Litel
Angela Merrova	Lya Lys
Pink	Huntz Hall
Detective Ray Kincaid	Charles Wilson
Miss Sweetman	Vera Lewis
Chairman	Howard Hickman
Undertaker	Olin Howland
Guide	Arthur Aylesworth
Detective Sgt. Moran	Jack Mower
Hotel Manager	Creighton Hale
Rodgers	John Ridgely
Editor	Joseph Crehan
Interne	Glenn Langan
Interne	William Hopper

SYNOPSIS

Investigating a series of deaths that leave the victims drained of blood, reporter Walter Barnett and interne Michael Rhodes are led to Dr. Francis Flegg, who experiments in restoring life to corpses through injections of rare Type One blood. Aiding Flegg is a mysterious "Doctor Xavier."

Actress Angela Merrova is found murdered, and every patient with Type One blood disappears from a hospital. Flegg himself in murdered, but before dying reveals that "Doctor Xavier" is Marshall Quesne, legally executed and buried, but brought back to life by Flegg's discoveries. The series of murders is due to Quesne's ceaseless search for blood to sustain his second life.

A hunt is started for Quesne, who has discovered that Joan Vance, a nurse and Rhodes' sweetheart, possesses the rare blood type he requires. Quesne lures Joan into a trap, but Barnett and Rhodes arrive with the police, who kill Quesne and save Joan from the fate of the others.

With Rosemary Lane

With Charles Wilson, Wayne Morris, Rosemary Lane, and Dennis Morgan

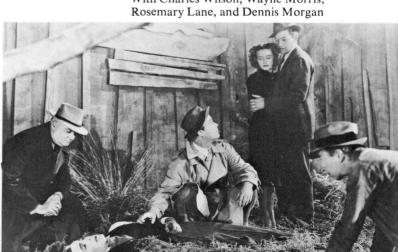

Invisible Stripes
1939

A Warner Bros.–First National Picture. Directed by Lloyd Bacon. Executive producer, Hal B. Wallis. Associate producer, Louis F. Edelman. Screenplay by Warren Duff. From an original story by Jonathan Finn, based on the book by Warden Lewis E. Lawes. Director of photography, Ernest Haller. Music by Heinz Roemheld. Film editor, James Gibbon. Dialogue director, Irving Rapper. Assistant director, Elmer Decker. Art director, Max Parker. Gowns by Milo Anderson. Make-up artist, Perc Westmore. Special effects by Byron Haskin. Sound recorder, Dolph Thomas. Orchestrations by Ray Heindorf. Running time, 82 minutes.

CAST

Cliff Taylor	GEORGE RAFT
Peggy	JANE BRYAN
Tim Taylor	WILLIAM HOLDEN
Chuck Martin	Humphrey BOGART
Mrs. Taylor	Flora ROBSON
Ed Kruger	Paul Kelly
Molly	Lee Patrick
Parole Officer Masters	Henry O'Neill
Tommy	Frankie Thomas
Warden	Moroni Olsen
Sue	Margot Stevenson
Lefty	Marc Lawrence
Johnny	Joseph Downing
Jimmy	Leo Gorcey
Shrank	William Haade
Old Peter	Tully Marshall

With George Raft

With William Holden and
George Raft

With George Raft and
Raymond Bailey

SYNOPSIS

Cliff Taylor and Chuck Martin are released from prison, Cliff intending to go straight, Chuck prepared to return to his old ways. As an ex-convict on parole, Cliff finds jobs hard to get; he is wearing invisible stripes. Finally, when he is making good, he is picked up on suspicion when the store where he works is robbed.

Cliff's brother Tim, struggling to make enough money to marry his sweetheart, Peggy, becomes discontented to the point of embarking on a criminal career. Risking his own freedom, Cliff joins Chuck and his gang in a series of bank robberies in order to buy a garage for his brother's security. When the money is sufficient Cliff quits the gang, alienating all but Chuck, with whom he parts friends.

Following a subsequent robbery the gang implicates Tim by using his garage as a getaway station. Chuck has been wounded during the holdup, and when Tim identifies the gangsters, Cliff goes to help Chuck get away before the police arrive. Cliff is followed by the other mobsters, who suspect him of informing, and as he and Chuck attempt to escape both are shot down.

With George Raft, Joseph Downing,
Marc Lawrence, and Paul Kelly

With Randolph Scott

Virginia City
1940

A Warner Bros.—First National Picture. Directed by Michael Curtiz. Executive producer, Hal B. Wallis. Associate producer, Robert Fellows. Original screenplay by Robert Buckner. Director of photography, Sol Polito. Music by Max Steiner. Film editor, George Amy. Dialogue director, Jo Graham. Assistant director, Sherry Shourds. Art director, Ted Smith. Makeup artist, Perc Westmore. Special effects by Byron Haskin and H. F. Koenekamp. Sound recorders, Oliver S. Garretson and Francis J. Scheid. Orchestrations by Hugo Friedhofer. Running time, 121 minutes.

With Russell Hicks, Randolph Scott, and George Regas

With Guinn "Big Boy" Williams,
Alan Hale and Errol Flynn

CAST

Kerry Bradford	ERROL FLYNN
Julia Hayne	MIRIAM HOPKINS
Vance Irby	Randolph SCOTT
John Murrell	Humphrey BOGART
Mr. Upjohn	Frank McHugh
Olaf Swenson	Alan Hale
Marblehead	Guinn "Big Boy" Williams
Marshall	John Litel
Major Drewery	Douglass Dumbrille
Dr. Cameron	Moroni Olsen
Armistead	Russell Hicks
Cobby	Dickie Jones
Union Soldier	Frank Wilcox
Gaylord	Russell Simpson
Abraham Lincoln	Victor Kilian
Jefferson Davis	Charles Middleton

SYNOPSIS

Kerry Bradford, a Union officer, escapes from the Confederate Libby Prison and is assigned to Virginia City, a Nevada mining town from which Southern sympathizers plan to ship $5,000,000 in gold to the tottering Confederacy. On the westbound stage Kerry meets Julia Hayne, a dance-hall entertainer also going to Virginia City. En route their stagecoach is held up by John Murrell, a half-breed outlaw.

In Virginia City Kerry finds that Vance Irby, former commandant of Libby Prison, plans to send the gold to Richmond by wagon train. Kerry falls in love with Julia, unaware that she is a Southern spy sent by Jefferson Davis to aid Vance. Julia sends Kerry into a trap and he is captured by Vance, who intends returning him to Libby Prison. Vance makes a deal with Murrell to have Murrell's bandits attack the Union garrison while his

With George Regas (right)

wagon train slips out of Virginia City.

As the bullion-laden caravan crosses the desert, it is stopped at a small Union outpost. When the soldiers attempt to inspect the wagons, the Southerners open fire and kill them. In the confusion, Kerry escapes and notifies Major Drewery, who arrives with a contingent of cavalry. While Drewery follows a false trail, Kerry and a few men catch up with Vance's caravan just as it is being attacked by Murrell's bandits, who have guessed its value. Kerry joins in defending the wagons and, dele-

gated command when Vance is killed, buries the gold to prevent its capture. The bandits are routed by the arrival of Drewery's cavalry, and Murrell is killed.

Kerry, considering it sufficient to block delivery of the gold, and hoping it will be used to help rebuild the post-war South, refuses to disclose its location to his superiors. He is court-martialed and sentenced to death, but Julia goes to the White House to plead for his life, and President Lincoln exercises executive clemency.

With Moroni Olsen, Paul Fix,
Randolph Scott, and George Regas

It All Came True

1940

A Warner Bros.–First National Picture. Directed by Lewis Seiler. Executive producer, Hal B. Wallis. Associate producer, Mark Hellinger. Screenplay by Michael Fessier and Lawrence Kimble. Based on the story "Better Than Life" by Louis Bromfield. Director of photography, Ernest Haller. Music by Heinz Roemheld. Film editor, Thomas Richards. Dialogue director, Robert Foulk. Assistant director, Russ Saunders. Art director, Max Parker. Gowns by Howard Shoup. Makeup artist, Perc Westmore. Special effects by Byron Haskin and Edwin B. DuPar. Sound recorder, Dolph Thomas. Dance director, Dave Gould. Songs: "Angel in Disguise" by Kim Gannon, Stephan Weiss, and Paul Mann; "The Gaucho Serenade" by James Cavanaugh, John Redmond and Nat Simon. Orchestral arrangements by Ray Heindorf and Frank Perkins. Running time, 97 minutes.

With Ann Sheridan

With Jeffrey Lynn

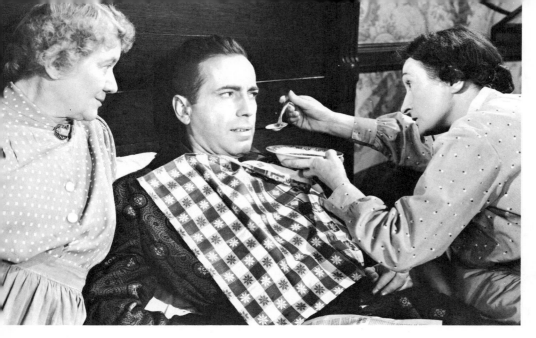

With Jessie Busley
and Una O'Connor

With Ann Sheridan

CAST

Sarah Jane Ryan	ANN SHERIDAN
Tommy Taylor	Jeffrey LYNN
Grasselli (Chips Maguire)	Humphrey BOGART
Miss Flint	ZaSu Pitts
Maggie Ryan	Una O'Connor
Norah Taylor	Jessie Busley
Mr. Roberts	John Litel
Mr. Salmon	Grant Mitchell
Mr. Boldini	Felix Bressart
Leantopopulos	Charles Judels
Mr. Van Diver	Brandon Tynan
Mr. Prendergast	Howard Hickman
Monks	Herbert Vigran

SYNOPSIS

Sarah Jane Ryan, a former night-club entertainer, and Tommy Taylor, a struggling songwriter, return home to a run-down boardinghouse presided over by their mothers, Maggie Ryan and Norah Taylor. With him Tommy brings "Mr. Grasselli," a fugitive gangster

With Jeffrey Lynn
and Ann Sheridan

With Jessie Busley

who has killed a policeman with Tommy's gun and whom Tommy must hide to protect himself. Tommy passes Grasselli off as a "nervous wreck" who must stay in his room, but Sarah Jane recognizes him as racketeer Chips Maguire, in whose club she once worked.

After a few days under the ministrations of Maggie and Norah, who try to mother the "invalid," Grasselli decides to take his chances downstairs in the parlor, where he witnesses an amateur show put on by Tommy, Sarah Jane, and the boarders. Grasselli suggests putting the boardinghouse on a paying basis by converting it into a nightclub, and Sarah Jane, although in love with Tommy, encourages Grasselli's attentions so he will help in the plan to pay off the taxes.

On a tip from Miss Flint, the housekeeper, the police catch up with Grasselli on the club's opening night. But the kindness shown him by the two old ladies and the other eccentric members of the ménage has made a sentimentalist of Grasselli, who clears Tommy, enabling the young lovers to make a clean start.

With Ann Sheridan

With Jessie Busley
and Jeffrey Lynn

83

With Ann Sheridan

Brother Orchid

1940

A Warner Bros.–First National Picture. Directed by Lloyd Bacon. Executive producer, Hal B. Wallis. Associate producer, Mark Hellinger. Screenplay by Earl Baldwin. Based on the Collier's *magazine story by Richard Connell. Director of photography, Tony Gaudio. Music by Heinz Roemheld. Film editor, William Holmes. Dialogue director, Hugh Cummings. Assistant director, Dick Mayberry. Art director, Max Parker. Gowns by Howard Shoup. Makeup artist, Perc Westmore. Special effects by Byron Haskin, Willard Van Enger, and Edwin B. DuPar. Montages by Don Siegel and Robert Burks. Sound recorder, C. A. Riggs. Orchestrations by Ray Heindorf. Running time, 91 minutes.*

CAST

Little John Sarto	EDWARD G. ROBINSON
Flo Addams	Ann SOTHERN
Jack Buck	Humphrey BOGART
Brother Superior	Donald Crisp
Clarence Fletcher	Ralph Bellamy
Willie the Knife	Allen Jenkins
Brother Wren	Charles D. Brown
Brother Goodwin	Cecil Kellaway
Philadelphia Powell	Morgan Conway
Mugsy O'Day	Richard Lane
Red Martin	Paul Guilfoyle
Texas Pearson	John Ridgely
Brother MacEwen	Joseph Crehan
Brother MacDonald	Wilfred Lucas
Curley Matthews	Tom Tyler
Buffalo Burns	Dick Wessel
Pattonsville Supt.	Granville Bates
French Frank	Paul Phillips
Al Muller	Don Rowan
Fifi	Nanette Vallon
Turkey Malone	Tim Ryan
Handsome Harry	Joe Caites
Dopey Perkins	Pat Gleason
Joseph	Tommy Baker

SYNOPSIS

Racket chieftain Little John Sarto, after a trip to Europe in search of "class," returns to find his mob taken over by his former associate, Jack Buck. Sarto organizes a new gang and muscles into his old territory. His girl friend, Flo Addams, attempting to promote peace between the rival factions, inadvertently sends Sarto into a trap, and Buck's gunmen take him for a

With Paul Phillips,
Morgan Conway, and
Edward G. Robinson

With Edward G. Robinson

ride. Wounded, Sarto escapes his would-be killers and manages to reach a monastery. Nursed back to health by the monks, Sarto at first cynically adopts the monastery as an ideal hideout, but he is affected by the selfless work and sincerity of the Brothers. Trying his hand at flower growing, he takes the name of Brother Orchid.

His regeneration is interrupted when he reads in the papers that Flo is to marry Clarence Fletcher, a hick rancher. He also learns that the Brothers are in a plight because Buck's "protective association" has banned the sale of the monastery's flowers. Sarto returns to the city and, with the help of Clarence and his visiting fellow ranchers, breaks up Buck's gang. Transformed by his life with the monks, Sarto leaves Flo to Clarence and returns to the monastery, where he has at last found real "class."

With Richard Lane, Edward G. Robinson, and Morgan Conway

They Drive By Night

1940

A Warner Bros.–First National Picture. Directed by Raoul Walsh. Executive producer, Hal B. Wallis. Associate producer, Mark Hellinger. Screenplay by Jerry Wald and Richard Macaulay. Based on the novel Long Haul by A. I. Bezzerides. Director of photography, Arthur Edeson. Music by Adolph Deutsch. Film editor, Thomas Richards. Dialogue director, Hugh MacMullen. Assistant director, Elmer Decker. Art director, John Hughes. Gowns by Milo Anderson. Makeup artist, Perc Westmore. Special effects by Byron Haskin, H. F. Koenekamp, James Gibbons, John Holden, and Edwin B. DuPar. Montages by Don Siegel and Robert Burks. Sound recorder, Oliver S. Garretson. Orchestrations by Arthur Lange. Running time, 93 minutes.

With George Raft and Ann Sothern

With Henry O'Neill

With Gale Page

CAST

With George Raft, Ann Sheridan,
Gale Page, and Roscoe Karns

With George Raft
and George Tobias

With George Raft

87

With Joyce Compton, Gale Page, Roscoe Karns, George Raft, and Ann Sheridan

SYNOPSIS

Brothers Joe and Paul Fabrini establish themselves in the trucking business. Most of the drivers work for Ed Carlsen, but Joe likes being independent and dreams of owning his own fleet of trucks. Paul, however, hates the road and longs for a more normal life with his wife, Pearl. The brothers pick up Cassie Hartley, a waitress hitchhiking to Los Angeles, and Joe falls for her. En route they see a truck, its driver asleep at the wheel, go off the road and explode in flames. Subsequently, Paul himself falls asleep while driving and in the ensuing accident loses an arm.

Joe goes to work for Ed Carlsen, attracting the at-tentions of Ed's wife, Lana, who influences her husband to make Joe his traffic manager. When Joe spurns her advances she kills Ed, disguising the crime as a drunken accident. She later gives Joe a half-interest in Ed's business in a further attempt to win him. When Joe tells her he is marrying Cassie she goes to the police, confesses, and accuses Joe of complicity in Ed's murder.

At the trial the weight of circumstantial evidence seems to doom Joe. But when Lana takes the stand her behavior reveals that she has become insane, and the case against Joe is dismissed. Joe returns to the trucking business he dreamed of owning, with Paul as his traffic manager and Cassie as his bride-to-be.

With Ann Sheridan and George Raft

High Sierra
1941

A Warner Bros.–First National Picture. Directed by Raoul Walsh. Executive producer, Hal B. Wallis. Associate producer, Mark Hellinger. Screenplay by John Huston and W. R. Burnett. Based on the novel by W. R. Burnett. Director of photography, Tony Gaudio. Music by Adolph Deutsch. Film editor, Jack Killifer. Dialogue director, Irving Rapper. Art director, Ted Smith. Gowns by Milo Anderson. Makeup artist, Perc Westmore. Special effects by Byron Haskin and H. F. Koenekamp. Sound recorder, Dolph Thomas. Orchestrations by Arthur Lange. Running time, 100 minutes.

With Ida Lupino

With Cornel Wilde, Arthur Kennedy, Ida Lupino, and Alan Curtis

With Henry Travers, Joan Leslie, Henry Hull, and Minna Gombell

With Ida Lupino

Marie Garson	IDA LUPINO
Roy Earle	HUMPHREY BOGART
Babe Kozak	Alan CURTIS
Red Hattery	Arthur KENNEDY
Velma	Joan LESLIE
Doc Banton	Henry HULL
Pa Goodhue	Henry TRAVERS
Healy	Jerome Cowan
Mrs. Baughman	Minna Gombell
Jake Kranmer	Barton MacLane
Ma Goodhue	Elisabeth Risdon
Louis Mendoza	Cornel Wilde
Big Mac	Donald MacBride
Mr. Baughman	Paul Harvey
Blonde	Isabel Jewell
Algernon	Willie Best
Ed	Spencer Charters
Pfiffer	George Meeker
Art	Robert Strange
Lon Preiser	John Eldredge
Announcer	Sam Hayes

With Joan Leslie

SYNOPSIS

Roy Earle is sprung from prison by Big Mac, an old gangland associate who wants him to go to California to engineer the holdup of a fashionable resort hotel. On the way Roy meets the Goodhues and their granddaughter, Velma, with whom he falls in love. Proceeding to a mountain hideout, Roy finds that Babe and Red, the henchmen assigned to him, have brought along a dance-hall girl, Marie. At first opposed to Marie's presence, Roy comes to trust her in preference to the men. He plans the holdup with the inside help of Louis Mendoza, a clerk at the hotel.

The holdup is pulled and Roy makes his getaway with Marie, but Babe and Red are killed when their car crashes. Mendoza talks, putting the police on Roy's trail. Roy goes to Big Mac but finds him dead of a heart attack. He then goes to Velma but finds her engaged to another man. Learning that the police are after him, he puts Marie on a bus and heads for one of the mountain passes out of California. His flight is halted by the police and, trapped on a mountain peak, he is killed.

With Arthur Kennedy,
Ida Lupino, and Alan Curtis

The Wagons Roll at Night

1941

A Warner Bros.–First National Picture. Directed by Ray Enright. Associate producer, Harlan Thompson. Screenplay by Fred Niblo, Jr. and Barry Trivers. Based on the novel Kid Galahad *by Francis Wallace. Director of photography, Sid Hickox. Music by Heinz Roem-* *held. Film editor, Frederick Richards. Assistant director, Jesse Hibbs. Art director, Hugh Reticker. Special effects by Byron Haskin and H. F. Koenekamp. Orchestrations by Ray Heindorf. Running time, 84 minutes.*

With Sylvia Sidney, John Ridgely, and Joan Leslie

With Joan Leslie and Eddie Albert

With Sylvia Sidney

With Eddie Albert and
Sig Rumann

With Cliff Clark, Joan Leslie
and Eddie Albert

CAST

Nick Coster	HUMPHREY BOGART
Flo Lorraine	SYLVIA SIDNEY
Matt Varney	Eddie ALBERT
Mary Coster	Joan LESLIE
Hoffman the Great	Sig Rumann
Doc	Cliff Clark
Snapper	Charley Foy
Tex	Frank Wilcox
Arch	John Ridgely
Mrs. Williams	Clara Blandick
Mr. Williams	Aldrich Bowker
Gus	Garry Owen
Bundy	Jack Mower
Wally	Frank Mayo

SYNOPSIS

A lion escapes from Nick Coster's traveling carnival and is cornered in a grocery store by clerk Matt Varney. Nick hires the boy and has him work with Hoffman the Great. In time Matt becomes a lion tamer and eventually replaces Hoffman, who is chronically drunk. After a fight with Hoffman, Matt is taken to Nick's farm by Flo Lorraine, the carnival's fortune-teller. Here he meets and falls in love with Mary Coster, Nick's young sister. Nick learns that Matt is on the farm and orders him back to the show, feeling that carnival people aren't good enough for his convent-bred sister.

When Matt ignores Nick's warning not to see Mary again, Nick plans to rid himself of the boy. He persuades Matt to make a quick reputation by going into the cage with Caesar, a mad lion kept only for exhibition purposes. Matt faces the beast courageously and puts up a losing battle until Nick, at the pleas of Flo and Mary, goes into the cage to rescue him. Matt is saved, but Nick is attacked by the insane lion and killed.

With Sylvia Sidney

With Eddie Albert

With Sylvia Sidney and Eddie Albert

With Sig Rumann

With Peter Lorre, Mary Astor, and Sydney Greenstreet

The Maltese Falcon
1941

With Mary Astor

A Warner Bros.–First National Picture. Directed by John Huston. Executive producer, Hal B. Wallis. Associate producer, Henry Blanke. Screenplay by John Huston. Based on the novel by Dashiell Hammett. Director of photography, Arthur Edeson. Music by Adolph Deutsch. Film editor, Thomas Richards. Dialogue director, Robert Foulk. Assistant director, Claude Archer. Art director, Robert Haas. Gowns by Orry-Kelly. Makeup artist, Perc Westmore. Sound recorder, Oliver S. Garretson. Orchestrations by Arthur Lange. Running time, 100 minutes.

CAST

Sam Spade	HUMPHREY BOGART
Brigid O'Shaughnessy	MARY ASTOR
Iva Archer	Gladys GEORGE
Joel Cairo	Peter LORRE
Lieutenant Dundy	Barton MacLane
Effie Perine	Lee Patrick
Casper Gutman	Sydney Greenstreet
Detective Tom Polhaus	Ward Bond
Miles Archer	Jerome Cowan
Wilmer Cook	Elisha Cook, Jr.
Luke	James Burke
Frank	Murray Alper
District Attorney Bryan	John Hamilton
Mate of the *La Paloma*	Emory Parnell
Captain Jacobi	Walter Huston

SYNOPSIS

Sam Spade and Miles Archer, partners in a private detective agency, are hired by a Miss Wonderly to shadow Floyd Thursby. Miles is killed while on the assignment, and Thursby is killed later the same night. Miss Wonderly, confessing that her real name is Brigid O'Shaughnessy, tells Spade that she is in danger and implores him to help her. He agrees to keep her name out of the case, his doubts mitigated by her beauty and her money.

Spade is visited by Joel Cairo, who offers him $5,000 to find a black statuette of a falcon. Spade reports the offer to Brigid, who asks for a meeting with Cairo. Here Spade learns of a third person, "the fat man," who also is interested in the falcon and whose gunsel, Wilmer, has been trailing him. Wilmer takes Spade to the fat

With Peter Lorre

With Mary Astor and Peter Lorre

With Mary Astor and Jerome Cowan

man, Casper Gutman, and Spade professes to know the falcon's whereabouts. But beyond scoffing at Cairo's offer, Gutman refuses to reveal any information about the black bird, and Spade storms out.

Brigid vanishes, and Wilmer summons Spade to a second meeting with Gutman. This time Gutman tells Spade the falcon's history and value but puts a drug in his drink, knocking him out. Recovering, Spade finds a clue which leads him to the ship *La Paloma,* but it is on fire when he arrives. Returning to his office, he is interrupted by the arrival of Captain Jacobi of the *La Paloma,* shot several times, who gives him the falcon and dies. Placing the falcon in a depot box, Spade goes to his apartment to find Brigid waiting outside and Gutman, Cairo, and Wilmer inside.

He learns from Gutman that Wilmer killed Thursby

With Mary Astor

With Elisha Cook, Jr., and
Sydney Greenstreet

With Lee Patrick and Mary Astor

With Mary Astor

and Jacobi and proposes that Wilmer be the fall guy, to which Gutman consents. After negotiating a price for the falcon, Spade has his secretary, Effie Perine, bring it to the apartment. Upon examination the statuette proves to be a fake, and during the excitement Wilmer escapes. Recovering from his disappointment, Gutman proposes to Cairo that they continue their search. Brigid remains with Spade, who telephones the police to pick up Gutman, Cairo, and Wilmer. Then, faced with the question of Miles' half-forgotten death, Spade deduces that it was Brigid herself who killed him. She confesses, but, citing their love, implores Spade not to send her over. But Spade won't "play the sap" for her; and he grimly hands her over to the police.

With Mary Astor

With Ward Bond, Mary Astor, and Barton MacLane

With Judith Anderson
and Frank McHugh

All Through the Night

1942

With William Demarest
and Kaaren Verne

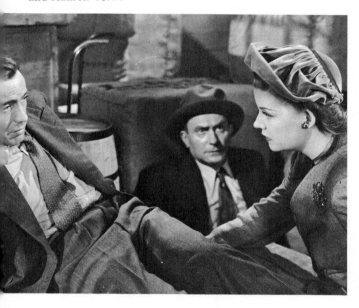

With James Burke (tall cop)
and Kaaren Verne (right)

A Warner Bros.–First National Picture. Directed by Vincent Sherman. Produced by Jerry Wald. Screenplay by Leonard Spigelgass and Edwin Gilbert. Based on an original story by Leonard Q. Ross (Leo Rosten) and Leonard Spigelgass. Director of photography, Sid Hickox. Music by Adolph Deutsch. Film editor, Rudi Fehr. Assistant director, William Kissel. Art director, Max Parker. Special effects by Edwin B. DuPar. Sound recorder, Oliver S. Garretson. Orchestrations by Frank Perkins. Song, "All Through the Night," by Johnny Mercer and Arthur Schwartz. Running time, 107 minutes.

CAST

Gloves Donahue	HUMPHREY BOGART
Hall Ebbing	CONRAD VEIDT
Leda Hamilton	KAAREN VERNE
Ma Donahue	Jane DARWELL
Barney	Frank McHUGH
Pepi	Peter LORRE
Madame	Judith ANDERSON
Sunshine	William Demarest
Starchie	Jackie Gleason
Waiter	Phil Silvers
Spats Hunter	Wallace Ford
Marty Callahan	Barton MacLane
Joe Denning	Edward Brophy
Steindorff	Martin Kosleck
Annabelle	Jean Ames
Mr. Miller	Ludwig Stossel
Mrs. Miller	Irene Seidner
Forbes	James Burke
Smitty	Ben Welden
Anton	Hans Schumm
Spence	Charles Cane
Sage	Frank Sully
Deacon	Sam McDaniel

With Martin Kosleck (right)

SYNOPSIS

Gloves Donahue, a big-shot Broadway gambler, sets out to find the killer of Mr. Miller, baker of Gloves' favorite cheesecake. He recognizes Leda Hamilton, a singer in Marty Callahan's night club, as the girl he saw leaving Miller's bakery. Joe Denning, Marty's partner, is mysteriously killed, and Leda and her accompanist, Pepi, disappear.

Suspected by Marty and the police of Joe's murder, Gloves traces Leda to an auction house operated by Hall Ebbing and his assistant, Madame. When he asks questions about Leda he is knocked out and imprisoned in a warehouse behind the auction rooms. Leda helps him escape, telling him that his captors are Nazi agents whom she is helping only to protect her father, a prisoner in Germany. When Gloves finds evidence that her father is dead, Leda reveals that Pepi killed Miller when he refused to aid the Nazis and killed Joe when he stumbled upon Pepi's identity.

Gloves and Leda go to the police, who search the warehouse but find it deserted. Disbelieving Gloves' story, the police arrest him, but he escapes and goes to his lawyer's apartment, where his cronies have gathered. They are interrupted by the arrival of Marty and his mob, eager to avenge Joe's murder. Gloves convinces them of his innocence, and leads the two gangs to the police station where Leda is being held. Ebbing, however, has bailed her out, and the gangs arrive as she is being forced into Ebbing's car.

They follow Ebbing to his hideout and break up the Nazis' headquarters, but Ebbing escapes, intending to carry out a prearranged plan to blow up a battleship in New York harbor. Gloves pursues him to the waterfront, where Ebbing gets the drop on him and forces him into a motorboat filled with high explosives. As Ebbing pilots his boat toward the battleship, Gloves seizes the wheel, veering the boat off its course and throwing Gloves into the water. Ebbing's boat crashes into a barge and explodes.

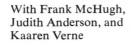

With Frank McHugh, Judith Anderson, and Kaaren Verne

100

With Irene Manning

The Big Shot
1942

A Warner Bros.–First National Picture. Directed by Lewis Seiler. Produced by Walter MacEwen. Original screenplay by Bertram Millhauser, Abem Finkel, and Daniel Fuchs. Director of photography, Sid Hickox. Music by Adolph Deutsch. Film editor, Jack Killifer. Dialogue director, Harold Winston. Assistant director, Art Lueker. Art director, John Hughes. Gowns by Milo Anderson. Makeup artist, Perc Westmore. Sound recorder, Stanley Jones. Orchestrations by Jerome Moross. Running time, 82 minutes.

With Chick Chandler

With Irene Manning

CAST

Duke Berne	HUMPHREY BOGART
Lorna Fleming	Irene MANNING
George Anderson	Richard TRAVIS
Ruth Carter	Susan PETERS
Martin Fleming	Stanley RIDGES
Warden Booth	Minor Watson
Dancer	Chick Chandler
Frenchy	Joseph Downing
Sandor	Howard da Silva
Quinto	Murray Alper
Faye	Roland Drew
Tim	John Ridgely
Toohey	Joseph King
Judge	John Hamilton
Mrs. Booth	Virginia Brissac
Sarto	William Edmunds
Mrs. Miggs	Virginia Sale
Kat	Ken Christy
Rusty	Wallace Scott

SYNOPSIS

Duke Berne, former big shot but now a three-time loser, fears returning to crime because a fourth conviction will mean a life sentence. Finally, haunted by his past and goaded by his cohorts, he joins in planning an armored car robbery. He learns that the gang is backed by a crack criminal attorney, Martin Fleming, and finds that Fleming's wife is his former sweetheart, Lorna, who is still in love with him. Lorna prevents Duke from joining in the holdup by keeping him in his room at gunpoint, but a flustered witness picks Duke out of a police mug-book, and he goes on trial. When a gang member informs Fleming that Duke and Lorna were together, Fleming exposes George Anderson, Duke's alibi, and both Duke and George are sentenced to prison.

Duke stages a prison break, during which a guard is killed. He meets Lorna, and they establish a brief idyll in a mountain hideout. But when Duke hears that George has been sentenced to death for the guard's murder, he decides to give himself up and clear George. As Duke and Lorna drive down the mountain road, the police arrive, tipped off by Fleming, and in the ensuing chase Lorna is killed. Duke gets away, goes to Fleming's apartment and kills him, but is mortally wounded by the dying attorney. With George and his girl friend, Ruth Carter, at his hospital bedside, Duke dies.

With Sydney Greenstreet

With Keye Luke and Mary Astor

Across the Pacific
1942

A Warner Bros.–First National Picture. Directed by John Huston. Produced by Jerry Wald and Jack Saper. Screenplay by Richard Macaulay. Based on the Saturday Evening Post *serial* Aloha Means Goodbye *by Robert Carson. Director of photography, Arthur Edeson. Music by Adolph Deutsch. Film editor, Frank Magee. Dialogue director, Edward Blatt. Assistant director, Lee Katz. Art directors, Robert Haas and Hugh Reticker. Gowns by Milo Anderson. Makeup artist, Perc Westmore. Special effects by Byron Haskin and Willard Van Enger. Montages by Don Siegel. Sound recorder, Everett A. Brown. Orchestrations by Clifford Vaughan. Running time, 97 minutes.*

With Rudy Robles
and Richard Loo

103

Rick Leland	HUMPHREY BOGART
Alberta Marlow	MARY ASTOR
Dr. Lorenz	SYDNEY GREENSTREET
A. V. Smith	Charles Halton
Joe Totsuiko	Victor Sen Yung
Sugi	Roland Got
Sam Wing On	Lee Tung Foo
Captain Morrison	Frank Wilcox
Colonel Hart	Paul Stanton
Canadian Major	Lester Matthews
Court-martial President	John Hamilton
Tall Thin Man	Tom Stevenson
Captain Harkness	Roland Drew
Dan Morton	Monte Blue
Captain Higoto	Chester Gan
First Officer Miyuma	Richard Loo
Steamship Office Clerk	Keye Luke
T. Oki	Kam Tong
Chief Engineer Mitsudo	Spencer Chan
Filipino Assassin	Rudy Robles

SYNOPSIS

Court-martialed out of the United States Army, Rick Leland attempts to enlist in the Canadian artillery but is rejected. At Halifax he takes passage on the *Genoa Maru,* a Japanese ship bound for Yokohama via New York and Panama. On board he meets Alberta Marlow, on her way to Panama, and Dr. Lorenz, an avowed admirer of the Japanese. He tells Lorenz of his dishonorable discharge and of his intention to sell his services to the highest bidder.

When the ship docks at New York, Rick reports to Army Intelligence headquarters, where he is revealed as a secret agent trailing Lorenz. As the *Genoa Maru*

With Mary Astor
and Sydney Greenstreet

proceeds toward Panama, Rick allows Lorenz to prod him into revealing details of the military installations guarding the Panama Canal. He also conducts a light-hearted romance with Alberta, and they fall in love.

In Panama Alberta disappears, and on a tip Rick goes to Dan Morton's Bountiful Plantation, where he is captured by guards. He finds Alberta and Morton, her father, held prisoners by Lorenz, who is using the plantation as a base from which to direct a bombing attack on the Canal. Overpowering his guard, Rick makes his way to a landing field, where a Japanese plane is being prepared to bomb the Gatun Locks. He captures a machine gun and shoots down the plane as it is about to take off. Returning to the plantation, he finds Lorenz preparing to commit hara-kiri, but the doctor has no stomach for the ritual and Rick takes him into custody.

With Mary Astor

With Philip Ahn

With Mary Astor, Lee Tung Foo, and Sydney Greenstreet

With Ingrid Bergman

With Paul Henreid, Ingrid Bergman and Claude Rains

Casablanca
1943

A Warner Bros.-First National Picture. Directed by Michael Curtiz. Produced by Hal B. Wallis. Screenplay by Julius J. & Philip G. Epstein and Howard Koch. Based on the play Everybody Comes to Rick's by Murray Burnett and Joan Alison. Director of photography, Arthur Edeson. Music by Max Steiner. Film editor, Owen Marks. Dialogue director, Hugh Mac-Mullen. Assistant director, Lee Katz. Art director, Carl Jules Weyl. Set decorations by George James Hopkins.

Gowns by Orry-Kelly. Makeup artist, Perc Westmore. Special effects by Lawrence Butler and Willard Van Enger. Montages by Don Siegel and James Leicester. Sound recorder, Francis J. Scheid. Orchestrations by Hugo Friedhofer. Songs: "As Time Goes By" by Herman Hupfeld; "Knock on Wood" by M. K. Jerome and Jack Scholl. Technical adviser, Robert Aisner. Narrated by Lou Marcelle. Running time, 102 minutes.

With Peter Lorre

CAST

Rick	HUMPHREY BOGART
Ilsa	INGRID BERGMAN
Victor Laszlo	PAUL HENREID
Captain Louis Renault	Claude RAINS
Major Strasser	Conrad VEIDT
Senor Farrari	SYDNEY GREENSTREET
Ugarte	Peter LORRE
Carl	S. Z. Sakall
Yvonne	Madeleine LeBeau
Sam	Dooley Wilson
Annina Brandel	Joy Page
Berger	John Qualen
Sascha	Leonid Kinsky
Jan Brandel	Helmut Dantine
Pickpocket	Curt Bois
Croupier	Marcel Dalio
Singer	Corinna Mura
Mr. Leuchtag	Ludwig Stossel
Mrs. Leuchtag	Ilka Gruning
Italian Officer Tonelli	Charles La Torre
Arab Vendor	Frank Puglia
Abdul	Dan Seymour

SYNOPSIS

Following the fall of France, refugees from Nazi-occupied Europe gather in Casablanca, where they attempt to obtain exit visas to Lisbon, take-off point for America. A favorite haunt of these refugees is Rick's Café Américain, owned by Richard Blaine, an enigmatic American who smuggled arms to Ethiopia and fought with the Loyalists in Spain but who, for the moment, refuses to "stick his neck out" for anyone.

With Ingrid Bergman

With Dooley Wilson

With Oliver Prickett
and Sydney Greenstreet

To Casablanca comes Major Heinrich Strasser, seeking the murderer of two German couriers who were carrying two precious letters of transit. Ugarte, who has the letters, prevails upon Rick to hide them for him briefly, but Ugarte is arrested by the police and later killed. Cooperating with Strasser is Casablanca's prefect of police, Captain Louis Renault, who, though no fascist, "blows with the wind."

Also in Casablanca are Victor Laszlo, a leader of Europe's underground, and his wife Ilsa, who need visas to continue Laszlo's work in America. In a flashback we learn that Ilsa and Rick had fallen in love in Paris and had planned to leave before the Nazis marched in, but that at the last moment Ilsa had deserted Rick.

With Ingrid Bergman

With Helmut Dantine (lower left)
and Marcel Dalio (center)

With Peter Lorre

108

The Laszlos attempt to obtain visas from Senor Ferrari, head of Casablanca's black market, but he refers them to Rick, whom he correctly believes has the letters of transit. While Laszlo is attending an underground meeting, Ilsa goes to Rick and pleads with him for the letters, but Rick, bitter over Ilsa's desertion in Paris, refuses to help. In desperation, Ilsa threatens to shoot Rick unless he gives her the letters, but she is still in love with him and cannot carry out her threat. She reveals that she was married to Laszlo when she met Rick, but, believing Laszlo dead in a German concentration camp, she permitted the Paris affair, and left Rick only when Laszlo turned up alive.

Rick tells Ilsa that they will use the letters themselves, and he deludes Renault into believing that he will set Laszlo up for arrest if he and Ilsa are allowed to leave Casablanca unmolested. Renault agrees but is crossed by Rick, who forces Renault to accompany him and the Laszlos to the airport, where he reveals that his real plans are to put the Laszlos on the Lisbon plane. Although Ilsa still loves Rick, she allows him to persuade her that Laszlo's work is more important, and she boards the plane with her husband.

Strasser, alerted by a furtive phone call from Renault, arrives at the airport and attempts to stop the flight. Rick shoots him, but he is saved from arrest by Renault, who, moved by Rick's *beau geste,* has at last become a patriot.

Casablanca opened at New York's Hollywood Theatre on Thanksgiving Day, 1942, only eighteen days after the Allied landings at Casablanca, and its general release date, January 23, 1943, came in the very midst of the Casablanca conference of Anglo-American leaders. Nothing could have been more timely. Its enormous success prompted several subsequent attempts to match its appeal—*Passage to Marseille, To Have and Have Not* and *Sirocco* all owed something to *Casablanca*—but none quite succeeded in capturing its unique flavor. The size and caliber of its international cast is still astonishing. Out of eight nominations, *Casablanca* won three Academy Awards: Best Screenplay, Best Directing, and Best Picture of 1943.

For Humphrey Bogart, *Casablanca* was also a great personal triumph. The role of "Rick" established him as a romantic star, brought him his first Academy Award nomination, and made him king of the Warner lot.

With Ingrid Bergman

With Dooley Wilson

With Paul Henreid and Ingrid Bergman

Action in the North Atlantic

1943

A Warner Bros.–First National Picture. Directed by Lloyd Bacon. Produced by Jerry Wald. Screenplay by John Howard Lawson. Additional dialogue by A. I. Bezzerides and W. R. Burnett. Based on the novel by Guy Gilpatric. Director of photography, Ted McCord. Music by Adolph Deutsch. Film editors, Thomas Pratt and George Amy. Dialogue director, Harold Winston. Assistant director, Reggie Callow. Art director, Ted Smith. Set decorations by Clarence I. Steensen. Gowns by Milo Anderson. Makeup artist, Perc Westmore. Special effects by Jack Cosgrove and Edwin B. DuPar. Montages by Don Siegel and James Leicester. Sound recorder, C. A. Riggs. Orchestrations by Jerome Moross. Running time, 127 minutes.

CAST

Joe Rossi	HUMPHREY BOGART
Captain Steve Jarvis	Raymond MASSEY
Boats O'Hara	Alan HALE
Pearl	Julie BISHOP
Mrs. Jarvis	Ruth GORDON
Chips Abrams	Sam Levene
Johnny Pulaski	Dane Clark
Whitey Lara	Peter Whitney
Cadet Robert Parker	Dick Hogan
Rear Admiral Hartridge	Minor Watson
Caviar Jinks	J. M. Kerrigan
Ensign Wright	Kane Richmond
German Sub Captain	William von Brincken
Goldberg	Chick Chandler
Cecil	George Offerman, Jr.
Lieutenant Commander	Don Douglas
Pete Larson	Art Foster
Aherne	Ray Montgomery
Tex Mathews	Glenn Strange
Sparks	Creighton Hale
Hennessy	Elliott Sullivan
McGonigle	Alec Craig
Captain Ziemer	Ludwig Stossel
Cherub	Dick Wessel
Captain Carpolis	Frank Puglia
Jenny O'Hara	Iris Adrian
Bartender	Irving Bacon
Lieutenant Commander	James Flavin

With Julie Bishop and Raymond Massey

With Sam Levene, Alan Hale and Raymond Massey

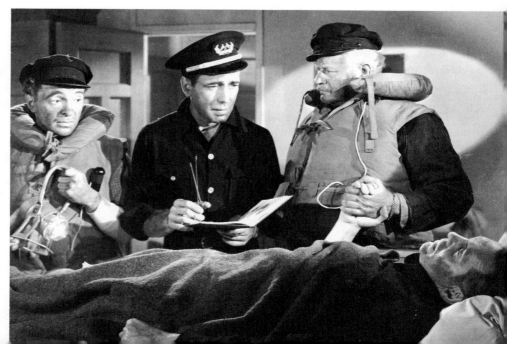

With Kane Richmond

SYNOPSIS

An American tanker is torpedoed and sunk by a German submarine, which then rams a lifeboat, forcing its occupants into the water. After eleven days at sea on a raft, the survivors are picked up and brought ashore to await assignment to a new ship. Captain Steve Jarvis returns home to his wife, while his first mate, Joe Rossi, meets a café singer named Pearl and marries her. Assigned to the *Sea Witch,* a new Liberty ship, Captain Jarvis takes Rossi on as his executive officer. Their ship is part of a convoy bound for Murmansk.

In the North Atlantic, German subs attack the convoy and the *Sea Witch* is separated from the other ships.

A submarine stalks the ship but cannot come within range because of the ship's guns. During the night the *Sea Witch* eludes the sub by shutting off its engines to prevent sonar detection. The U-boat notifies the *Luftwaffe,* and the following day the *Sea Witch* is attacked by two enemy planes, which kill several seamen and wound Captain Jarvis before being shot down. Rossi takes command, but the *Sea Witch* is again picked up by the German submarine. By faking a fire aboard ship, Rossi lures the sub to the surface and rams it. A squadron of Russian planes appears and escorts the *Sea Witch,* its valuable cargo intact, into Murmansk.

With Dane Clark

111

Thank Your Lucky Stars

1943

With S. Z. Sakall

With Matt McHugh and S. Z. Sakall

A Warner Bros.–First National Picture. Directed by David Butler. Produced by Mark Hellinger. Screenplay by Norman Panama & Melvin Frank and James V. Kern. Based on an original story by Everett Freeman and Arthur Schwartz. Director of photography, Arthur Edeson. Film editor, Irene Morra. Dialogue director, Herbert Farjean. Assistant director, Phil Quinn. Art directors, Anton Grot and Leo K. Kuter. Set decorations by Walter F. Tilford. Gowns by Milo Anderson. Makeup artist, Perc Westmore. Special effects by H. F. Koenekamp. Sound recorders, Francis J. Scheid and Charles David Forrest. Dance numbers created and staged by Leroy Prinz. Songs by Arthur Schwartz and Frank Loesser. Orchestral arrangements by Ray Heindorf. Vocal arrangements by Dudley Chambers. Musical adaptation by Heinz Roemheld. Orchestrations by Maurice de Packh. Running time, 127 minutes.

CAST

Himself	HUMPHREY BOGART
Himself and Joe Simpson	EDDIE CANTOR
Herself	BETTE DAVIS
Herself	OLIVIA DE HAVILLAND
Himself	ERROL FLYNN
Himself	JOHN GARFIELD
Pat Dixon	JOAN LESLIE
Herself	IDA LUPINO
Tom Randolph	DENNIS MORGAN
Herself	ANN SHERIDAN
Herself	DINAH SHORE
Herself	ALEXIS SMITH
Himself	Jack Carson
Himself	Alan Hale
Himself	George Tobias
Farnsworth	Edward Everett Horton
Dr. Schlenna	S. Z. Sakall
Gossip	Hattie McDaniel
Nurse Hamilton	Ruth Donnelly
Announcer	Don Wilson
Soldier	Willie Best
Angelo	Henry Armetta
Girl with a book	Joyce Reynolds

Spike Jones and His City Slickers

SYNOPSIS

Farnsworth and Schlenna, producing a Calvalcade of Stars benefit, find they must accept Eddie Cantor as chairman of the show in order to get his vocalist, Dinah Shore. At the first rehearsal Cantor takes over, disrupting all the producers' plans.

Singer Tom Randolph, who thinks he is to be on the show, finds he has been sold a phony contract by a crooked agent who has also rooked a young song writer, Pat Dixon. Chasing the agent, Pat runs into a bus driver named Joe Simpson, a would-be actor who can't break into show business because he looks too much like Eddie Cantor. Joe takes Pat to Gower Gulch, a colony inhabited by Hollywood's "cowboys" and "Indians," where she and Tom meet.

The young performers concoct a scheme to get themselves and Joe a chance on the show and rid the producers of the meddlesome Cantor as well. They have a trio of Gower Gulch Indians kidnap Cantor and induct him into their tribe, while Joe impersonates Cantor and gets the show under way.

After a number of escapades, Cantor evades his abductors and breaks into the theater. Rising to the occasion, Joe successfully convinces everyone, including two of Cantor's own stooges, that he is the real Cantor, and the "imposter" is thrown out. The show goes on to a triumphant finale, with Joe standing before the footlights to take his bows along with the assembled stars.

Sahara
1943

A Columbia Picture. Directed by Zoltan Korda. Produced by Harry Joe Brown. Screenplay by John Howard Lawson and Zoltan Korda. Adaptation by James O'Hanlon. From an original story by Philip MacDonald, based on an incident in the Soviet film The Thirteen. *Director of photography, Rudolph Maté. Music by Miklos Rozsa. Film editor, Charles Nelson. Assistant director, Abby Berlin. Art director, Lionel Banks; associate, Eugene Lourie. Set decorations by William Kiernan. Sound recorder, Lodge Cunningham. Musical director, Morris Stoloff. Running time, 97 minutes.*

With Carl Harbord

With Richard Nugent, Louis Mercier, Guy Kingsford, Patrick O'Moore, Carl Harbord and Lloyd Bridges

With Patrick O'Moore

CAST

Sergeant Joe Gunn	HUMPHREY BOGART
Waco Hoyt	Bruce Bennett
Giuseppe	J. Carrol Naish
Fred Clarkson	Lloyd Bridges
Tambul	Rex Ingram
Capt. Jason Halliday	Richard Nugent
Jimmy Doyle	Dan Duryea
Marty Williams	Carl Harbord
Ozzie Bates	Patrick O'Moore
Jean Leroux	Louis Mercier
Peter Stegman	Guy Kingsford
Capt. Von Schletow	Kurt Krueger
Major Von Falken	John Wengraf
Sergeant Krause	Hans Schumm

SYNOPSIS

After the fall of Tobruk, an American tank crew attached to the British Eighth Army is cut off by the advancing Germans. Heading south across the Libyan Desert to rejoin their command, Sergeant Joe Gunn and his crew pick up five British stragglers, a Free Frenchman, and a Sudanese corporal with his Italian prisoner. When a German plane strafes them, they shoot it down and capture the pilot.

In search of water, they are led by the Sudanese to an old fort, but they find the well nearly dry. As they wait patiently for a thin trickle of water to replenish their supply, they are overtaken by a pursuing German motorized battalion. They capture an advance scout car and learn from the prisoners that the Germans too are badly in need of water. Gunn decides to hold off the Germans, who are unaware that the well is now dry.

Repeated attacks by the Germans decimate the defenders until only Gunn and a single British soldier are left alive. What appears to be a final assault turns out to be a mass surrender as the thirst-crazed Germans throw down their arms in return for water. Ironically, a German shell has made a direct hit on the well, reopening it and providing water for all.

With Bruce Bennett, Dan Duryea,
Lloyd Bridges, and Richard Nugent

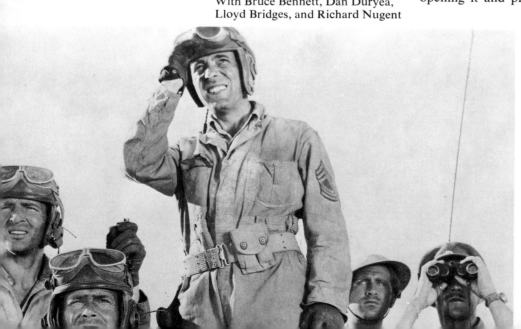

With Helmut Dantine, George Tobias,
Billy Roy and Philip Dorn

Passage to Marseille

1944

A Warner Bros.–First National Picture. Directed by Michael Curtiz. Produced by Hal B. Wallis. Screenplay by Casey Robinson and Jack Moffitt. Based on the novel Men Without Country by Charles Nordhoff and James Norman Hall. Director of photography, James Wong Howe. Music by Max Steiner. Film editor, Owen Marks. Dialogue director, Herschel Daugherty. Assistant director, Frank Heath. Art director, Carl Jules Weyl. Set decorations by George James Hopkins. Gowns by Leah Rhodes. Makeup artist, Perc Westmore. Special effects by Jack Cosgrove, Edwin B. DuPar, Byron Haskin, E. Roy Davidson, and Rex Wimpy. Montages by James Leicester. Sound recorder, Everett A. Brown. Orchestrations by Leonid Raab. Song, "Someday I'll Meet You Again," by Max Steiner and Ned Washington. Technical adviser, Sylvain Robert. Running time, 109 minutes.

With Michele Morgan

With Michele Morgan

With George Tobias and Peter Lorre

SYNOPSIS

At an air base in England, Manning, a newspaperman seeking material on the Free French, and Captain Freycinet, liaison officer between French and English, watch as French bomber crews prepare for a raid. Manning's attention is drawn to Matrac, a gunner, and Freycinet tells him Matrac's story:

A French journalist who opposed the Munich Pact, Matrac is framed on a murder charge and imprisoned on Devil's Island. He and four other convicts—Renault, Marius, Petit, and Garou—escape in a canoe and are picked up by a French freighter under Captain Malo. They are befriended by Freycinet, a passenger on the ship, whom they tell of their dedication to return to

With Vladimir Sokoloff,
George Tobias, Peter Lorre,
Helmut Dantine, and
Philip Dorn

With convicts Peter Lorre,
Helmut Dantine, George Tobias,
Philip Dorn; mess boy Billy Roy;
officers Konstantin Shayne,
Monte Blue, Victor Francen,
Eduardo Cianelli

fight for France. En route to Marseilles, the ship receives news of France's surrender. Major Duval, a fascist sympathizer, leads a plot to seize the ship and turn it over to Vichy, but the convicts aid in suppressing the mutiny. The ship reaches England, where the convicts join a Free French bomber squadron.

As Freycinet finishes his tale, the squadron returns from its raid over France. Renault's plane is delayed, for he has received permission to deviate from his course so that Matrac may drop a letter to his wife, Paula, and a son whom he has never seen. Renault's bomber, badly shot up, finally lands. Matrac has been killed, and as Freycinet and Manning watch, his body is taken from the plane.

Report from the Front
1944

Prepared by the Red Cross Drive Committee of the Motion Picture Industry. Distributed by National Screen Service. Running time, 3 minutes.

Bogart, accompanied by his (third) wife, Mayo Methot, arrived in North Africa on December 11, 1943, to begin a three-month tour entertaining American troops. They visited camps, bases, hospitals, and field units in Africa and Italy, presenting a short variety show. *Report from the Front,* an outgrowth of that tour, was prepared for Motion Picture Theatres Red Cross Week (March 23-29, 1944). This special trailer was made available without charge to all theatres signing pledges of participation, and was distributed through National Screen Service exchanges. Bogart appeared with his wife in film clips from their tour, spoke the narration accompanying scenes of actual fighting, and made an appeal for donations which were collected in each theatre at the conclusion of the trailer.

With Lauren Bacall

To Have and

With Walter Brennan

A Warner Bros.–First National Picture. Produced and directed by Howard Hawks. Screenplay by Jules Furthman and William Faulkner. Based on the novel by Ernest Hemingway. Director of photography, Sid Hickox. Music by Franz Waxman. Film editor, Christian Nyby. Assistant director, Jack Sullivan. Art director, Charles Novi. Set decorations by Casey Roberts. Gowns by Milo Anderson. Makeup artist, Perc Westmore. Special effects by E. Roy Davidson and Rex Wimpy. Sound recorder, Oliver S. Garretson. Orchestrations by Leonid Raab. Songs: "How Little We Know" by Hoagy Carmichael and Johnny Mercer; "Hong Kong Blues" by Hoagy Carmichael and Stanley Adams; "Am I Blue?" by Harry Akst and Grant Clarke. Technical adviser, Louis Comien. Running time, 100 minutes.

With Dolores Moran, Marcel Dalio, Lauren Bacall, Dan Seymour, and Sheldon Leonard

With Walter Sande
and Walter Brennan

Have Not

1945

CAST

Harry Morgan	HUMPHREY BOGART
Eddie	Walter BRENNAN
Marie	Lauren BACALL
Helene de Brusac	Dolores MORAN
Cricket	Hoagy CARMICHAEL
Paul de Brusac	Walter Molnar
Lieutenant Coyo	Sheldon Leonard
Gerard	Marcel Dalio
Johnson	Walter Sande
Captain Renard	Dan Seymour
Renard's Bodyguard	Aldo Nadi
Beauclerc	Paul Marion
Mrs. Beauclerc	Patricia Shay
Bartender	Emmett Smith
Horatio	Sir Lancelot

With Lauren Bacall

With Walter Brennan,
Dan Seymour, and
Sheldon Leonard

With Eugene Borden

SYNOPSIS

On the island of Martinique in the days following the fall of France, Harry Morgan, skipper of a small cabin cruiser, hires out his boat to wealthy sportsmen. Returning from a fishing trip with his current client, Johnson, Morgan is approached by Gerard, his hotel-keeper and a de Gaullist, who wants him to smuggle in a French underground leader. Unwilling to become embroiled in politics, Morgan refuses.

An American girl, Marie, arrives at the hotel, en route from Trinidad to the States, and she and Morgan enter into a caustic flirtation. While attempting to collect his fee from Johnson, Morgan is caught in a Vichy police raid at the hotel café. Johnson is killed by a stray bullet and Morgan's funds are impounded by the police.

To buy a ticket for Marie's plane trip back to America, and because he's broke himself, Morgan agrees to undertake the de Gaullist's mission. With Eddie, a derelict rummy whom he takes care of, Morgan picks up the underground leader and his wife, Paul and

With Walter Sande
and Lauren Bacall

With Dan Seymour, Aldo Nadi,
Sheldon Leonard, Marcel Dalio,
and Lauren Bacall

Helene de Brusac, from a nearby islet. On the way back, Morgan has a brush with a Vichy patrol boat and Brusac is wounded.

Delivering his passengers to Gerard's hotel, Morgan finds Marie singing in the café, with Cricket, the café's piano player. She has not used the plane ticket. In the cellar of the hotel, Morgan removes the bullet from Brusac's shoulder. Expecting trouble from the police, he tells Marie to pack for a quick flight, but when they are ready to leave he cannot find Eddie. He is visited by Captain Renard and Lieutenant Coyo, of the Vichy police, who reveal that they are holding Eddie for questioning, knowing he will talk if liquor is withheld from him.

Morgan's reaction is explosive. He shoots Renard's bodyguard and pistol-whips Renard and Coyo into telephoning for Eddie's release. Turning the police over to the de Gaullists, Morgan leaves Fort de France with Eddie and Marie.

With Dan Seymour and Louis Mercier

With Lauren Bacall

With Lauren Bacall,
Marcel Dalio, Walter Molnar
(on bed), and Dolores Moran
(on floor)

Conflict

1945

A Warner Bros.–First National Picture. Directed by Curtis Bernhardt. Produced by William Jacobs. Screenplay by Arthur T. Horman and Dwight Taylor. Based on an original story by Robert Siodmak and Alfred Neumann. Director of photography, Merritt Gerstad. Music by Frederick Hollander. Film editor, David Weisbart. Dialogue director, James Vincent. Assistant director, Elmer Decker. Art director, Ted Smith. Set decorations by Clarence I. Steensen. Gowns by Milo Anderson. Makeup artist, Perc Westmore. Sound recorder, Oliver S. Garretson. Orchestrations by Jerome Moross. Running time, 86 minutes.

CAST

Richard Mason	HUMPHREY BOGART
Evelyn Turner	ALEXIS SMITH
Dr. Mark Hamilton	SYDNEY GREENSTREET
Kathryn Mason	Rose Hobart
Prof. Norman Holdsworth	Charles Drake
Dr. Grant	Grant Mitchell
Detective Lt. Egan	Patrick O'Moore
Nora Grant	Ann Shoemaker
Robert Freston	Frank Wilcox
Phillips	Edwin Stanley
Detective Lt. Workman	James Flavin
Mrs. Allman	Mary Servoss

With Rose Hobart, Sidney Greenstreet, Charles Drake, and Alexis Smith

With Alexis Smith

SYNOPSIS

Richard and Kathryn Mason, whose friends believe them to be happily married, quarrel as they dress for a dinner celebrating their fifth wedding anniversary. Mason admits loving Kathryn's younger sister, Evelyn, but Kathryn refuses to give him up. Returning home from the dinner, hosted by psychiatrist Mark Hamilton, Mason suffers a leg injury in an auto accident. Although he recovers in a few weeks, he conceals the fact that he can walk and declines to accompany Kathryn on a trip to a mountain resort. On a lonely mountain road, Mason intercepts Kathryn, kills her, and pushes her car over a cliff. He returns home unseen, resumes his pose as an invalid, and reports his wife missing.

A series of strange incidents causes Mason to doubt Kathryn's death. He is harried by the odor of her perfume, the reappearance of jewelry she wore when she died, an envelope addressed in her handwriting. Mason pays troubled court to Evelyn, but she rejects his advances, claiming that Kathryn's memory stands between them. When Mason thinks he sees Kathryn on the street, he begins to question his sanity. To convince himself that Kathryn is dead he returns to the scene of his crime, only to find Dr. Hamilton and the police waiting for him. The incidents were contrived by the police to trap him after Hamilton spotted a flaw in his description of Kathryn as he last saw her. He described her as wearing a rose—a rose given her by Hamilton when she stopped at his house on her way to the mountain resort.

With Sydney Greenstreet

Hollywood Victory Caravan

1945

Produced for the War Activities Committee and the Treasury Department by Paramount Pictures. War Activities Committee release No. 136. Directed by William Russell. Produced by Louis Harris. Supervisor, Bernard Luber. Script by Melville Shavelson. Song, "We've Got Another Bond to Buy," by Jimmy McHugh and Harold Adamson. Running time, 20 minutes.

CAST

Robert Benchley, Humphrey Bogart, Joe Carioca, Carmen Cavallero and his orchestra, Bing Crosby, William Demarest, Dona Drake, Bob Hope, Betty Hutton, Alan Ladd, Diana Lynn, Noreen Nash, Franklin Pangborn, Olga San Juan, Barbara Stanwyck, Charles Victor, Marjorie Weaver, Virginia Welles, and the U.S. Maritime Service Training Station Choir.

The story concerned the desire of a war hero's sister to meet him in Washington and her adventures while trying to join a trainload of stars headed for a Washington rally. Bogart delivered an appeal for Victory Loan bonds.

Two Guys from Milwaukee

1946

A Warner Bros.–First National Picture. Directed by David Butler. Produced by Alex Gottlieb. Original screenplay by Charles Hoffman and I. A. L. Diamond. Director of photography, Arthur Edeson. Music by Frederick Hollander. Film editor, Irene Morra. Dialogue director, Felix Jacoves. Assistant director, Jesse Hibbs. Art director, Leo K. Kuter. Set decorations by Jack McConaghy. Gowns by Leah Rhodes. Makeup artist, Perc Westmore. Special effects by Harry Barndollar and Edwin B. DuPar. Montages by James Leicester. Sound recorder, Stanley Jones. Orchestrations by Leonid Raab. Song, "And Her Tears Flowed Like Wine," by Charles Lawrence, Joe Greene, and Stan Kenton. Running time, 90 minutes.

CAST

Prince Henry	DENNIS MORGAN
Buzz Williams	JACK CARSON
Connie Reed	JOAN LESLIE
Polly	Janis PAIGE
Count Oswald	S. Z. SAKALL
Peggy	Patti BRADY
Happy	Tom D'Andrea
Nan	Rosemary DeCamp
Mike Collins	John Ridgely
Johnson	Pat McVey
Theatre Manager	Franklin Pangborn
Dr. Bauer	Francis Pierlot
Herself	Lauren Bacall
Himself	Humphrey Bogart

SYNOPSIS

Henry, a Balkan prince visiting the United States, sheds his identity at an official New York reception and goes out on his own to see the "real" America. He has two desires—to meet his dream girl, Lauren Bacall, and to meet the "common man." He strikes up an acquaintance with the first common man he sees, a cab driver named Buzz Williams. Prince Henry has only two days until he must deliver a radio address to his subjects, who are holding a plebiscite, but in this time Buzz gives him a liberal education in the ways of America and Americans.

The police locate Prince Henry and bring him back in time for his radio address. As Henry and Buzz compare the advantages of a democracy over a monarchy, a mike is switched on the air ahead of schedule and Buzz's plea for democracy is heard by Prince Henry's subjects, who vote for a republic in their plebiscite, putting the Prince out of a job.

Henry accepts a job as a brewery salesman and boards a plane for Milwaukee. He takes a seat next to an attractive young lady who, to his surprise, is his dream girl, Lauren Bacall. But a tap on the shoulder makes Henry's elation short-lived as his seat is claimed by a dour-faced Humphrey Bogart.

With Lauren Bacall

The Big Sleep
1946

A Warner Bros.–First National Picture. Produced and directed by Howard Hawks. Screenplay by William Faulkner, Leigh Brackett, and Jules Furthman. Based on the novel by Raymond Chandler. Director of photography, Sid Hickox. Music by Max Steiner. Film editor, Christian Nyby. Assistant director, Robert Vreeland. Art director, Carl Jules Weyl. Set decorations by Fred M. MacLean. Gowns by Leah Rhodes. Special effects by E. Roy Davidson, Warren E. Lynch, William McGann, Robert Burks, and Willard Van Enger. Sound recorder, Robert B. Lee. Orchestrations by Simon Bucharoff. Running time, 114 minutes.

With Trevor Bardette and Bob Steele

With Lauren Bacall, Sonia Darrin, and Louis Jean Heydt

With Dorothy Malone

CAST

Philip Marlowe	HUMPHREY BOGART
Vivian Rutledge	LAUREN BACALL
Eddie Mars	John Ridgely
Carmen Sternwood	Martha Vickers
Bookshop Proprietress	Dorothy Malone
Mrs. Eddie Mars	Peggy Knudsen
Bernie Ohls	Regis Toomey
General Sternwood	Charles Waldron
Norris	Charles D. Brown
Canino	Bob Steele
Harry Jones	Elisha Cook, Jr.
Joe Brody	Louis Jean Heydt
Agnes	Sonia Darrin
Captain Cronjager	James Flavin
District Attorney Wilde	Thomas Jackson
Carol Lundgren	Dan Wallace
Arthur Gwynn Geiger	Theodore Von Eltz
Taxicab Driver	Joy Barlowe
Sidney	Tom Fadden
Pete	Ben Welden
Art Huck	Trevor Bardette
Medical Examiner	Joseph Crehan

With Martha Vickers

With Lauren Bacall
and Paul Webber

With Charles D. Brown
and Charles Waldron

With Lauren Bacall and Bob Steele

SYNOPSIS

Private detective Philip Marlowe is hired by General Sternwood to rid him of a blackmailer, Arthur Gwynn Geiger, who is peddling nude photographs of Sternwood's nymphomaniac daughter, Carmen. Marlowe finds Geiger murdered, killed by Sternwood's chauffeur, who was sweet on Carmen. Geiger's stock of pornography disappears from his bookshop, and Marlowe traces it to Joe Brody, boy friend of Geiger's clerk, Agnes. Brody tries to sell Carmen's photographs to her sister, Vivian, but he is killed by Carol Lundgren, Geiger's gunsel, who wrongly believes that Brody killed his "queen." Marlowe captures Lundgren and turns him over to Detective Bernie Ohls of the police.

Vivian tries to talk Marlowe off the case, but he is interested in Geiger's landlord, gambler Eddie Mars, at whose casino Vivian frequently plays. Marlowe is further intrigued when he learns that Mrs. Mars is missing, supposedly having run off with a former friend of General Sternwood's, Sean Regan. Outside Eddie's casino, Marlowe saves Vivian from a holdup man who tries to rob her of her winnings. Marlowe is approached by Agnes' new boy friend, Harry Jones, who offers to lead

With James Flavin, Regis Toomey,
and Thomas Jackson

With Bob Steele

him to Mrs. Mars, but Jones is killed by Eddie's trig-german, Canino. Agnes sends Marlowe to Art Huck's garage, where he is captured by Canino, who is holed up with Mrs. Mars. Vivian is there too, and in Canino's absence she releases Marlowe. When Canino returns, Marlowe kills him.

Taking Vivian with him, Marlowe makes an appointment with Eddie at Geiger's house. Eddie arrives and stations his men outside, but when he enters he finds Marlowe already there, waiting for him. Marlowe faces Eddie with his deductions: Eddie hid his wife out, with Canino guarding her, to let people think she had run away with Sean Regan. But Regan probably is dead, killed by Carmen when he wouldn't give her a tumble;

Carmen is like that. To protect her sister, Vivian asked Eddie for help and he gave it, but Vivian paid him blackmail—when she lost at his casino, she lost; when she won, Eddie sent a gunman to "rob" her of her winnings. Eddie had Canino kill Jones when Jones found Mrs. Mars, and he tried to have Marlowe killed too when he found the hideout.

Eddie admits all this, knowing that Marlowe has no proof and that his men will shoot Marlowe down as he leaves the house anyway. But Marlowe knows this too. He forces Eddie outside at gunpoint, where Eddie is machine-gunned by his own men. Phoning for the police, Marlowe waits with Vivian for them to arrive.

With Lauren Bacall and Martha Vickers

128

With Lizabeth Scott

With Lizabeth Scott

Dead Reckoning
1947

A Columbia Picture. Directed by John Cromwell. Produced by Sidney Biddell. Screenplay by Oliver H. P. Garrett and Steve Fisher. Adaptation by Allen Rivkin. Based on an original story by Gerald Adams and Sidney Biddell. Director of photography, Leo Tover. Music by Marlin Skiles. Assistant director, Seymour Friedman. Art directors, Stephen Goosson and Rudolph Sternad. Set decorations by Louis Diage. Gowns by Jean Louis. Makeup artist, Clay Campbell. Hair styles by Helen Hunt. Sound recorder, Jack Goodrich. Song, "Either It's Love or It Isn't," by Allan Roberts and Doris Fisher. Musical director, Morris Stoloff. Running time, 100 minutes.

CAST

Rip Murdock	HUMPHREY BOGART
Coral Chandler	LIZABETH SCOTT
Martinelli	Morris Carnovsky
Lieutenant Kincaid	Charles Cane
Johnny Drake	William Prince
Krause	Marvin Miller
McGee	Wallace Ford
Father Logan	James Bell
Louis Ord	George Chandler
Lt. Col. Simpson	William Forrest
Hyacinth	Ruby Dandridge

With Morris Carnovsky
and Marvin Miller

SYNOPSIS

Two paratroopers, Rip Murdock and Johnny Drake, are en route to Washington when Johnny disappears, and later is found murdered. Tracing Johnny's past, Rip learns that he was once accused of murder and that a witness against him at the inquest, Louis Ord, is now a waiter in Martinelli's night club. While at the club to see Ord, Rip meets Coral Chandler, for whose love Johnny is supposed to have murdered her husband. Rip falls in love with Coral, who seems devoted to Johnny's memory and eager to aid Rip in his investigation.

When Ord is murdered, Rip suspects Martinelli of being involved and attempts to rifle his safe for clues, but he is caught and beaten by Martinelli's sadistic henchman, Krause. He escapes and goes to Coral's apartment, where he accuses her of killing her husband. Coral confesses but pleads self-defense, saying that Johnny insisted on taking the blame and that Martinelli, in whom she confided, is blackmailing her. Rip, still in love with her, believes in her innocence and asks her to drive him to Martinelli's for another try, this time for the murder gun.

Rip forces Martinelli to hand over the murder weapon, but Martinelli dashes from the club and is shot down by Coral. Driving away with Coral, Rip accuses her of thinking that she was shooting him instead of Martinelli, and tells her that he is going to turn her over to the police. Coral demands that he give her the gun she used to kill her husband, but he refuses. Coral shoots him and the car crashes. Rip survives to clear Johnny's name, but Coral, gripping Rip's hand like a frightened child, dies in the hospital from her injuries.

With Lizabeth Scott

With Marvin Miller,
Lizabeth Scott, and
Morris Carnovsky

With Barbara Stanwyck

The Two Mrs. Carrolls
1947

A Warner Bros.–First National Picture. Directed by Peter Godfrey. Produced by Mark Hellinger. Screenplay by Thomas Job. Based on the play by Martin Vale. Director of photography, Peverell Marley. Music by Franz Waxman. Film editor, Frederick Richards. Assistant director, Claude Archer. Art director, Anton Grot. Set decorations by Budd Friend. Gowns by Edith Head and Milo Anderson. Makeup artist, Perc Westmore. Special effects by Robert Burks. Sound recorder, C. A. Riggs. Orchestrations by Leonid Raab. Running time, 99 minutes.

CAST

Geoffrey Carroll	HUMPHREY BOGART
Sally Carroll	BARBARA STANWYCK
Cecily Latham	ALEXIS SMITH
Dr. Tuttle	Nigel BRUCE
Mrs. Latham	Isobel Elsom
Charles Pennington	Patrick O'Moore
Beatrice Carroll	Ann Carter
Christine	Anita Bolster
Mr. Blagdon	Barry Bernard
MacGregor	Colin Campbell
Race Track Tout	Peter Godfrey

With Barbara Stanwyck

With Alexis Smith

SYNOPSIS

Geoffrey Carroll, an American artist living in London, completes a portrait of his wife as "The Angel of Death." Her usefulness as his model ended, Geoffrey slowly murders her by poisoning her milk.

With his second wife, Sally, and his young daughter, Beatrice, Geoffrey moves to the cathedral town of Ashton, where he begins Sally's portrait. He finds inspiration for still a third portrait when he falls in love with a neighbor, Cecily Latham. He begins the slow process of poisoning Sally, but he is blackmailed by Blagdon, the druggist from who he obtains the poison. Cecily, ignorant of Geoffrey's plan to dispose of Sally, believes he is putting her off and threatens to leave him unless he goes away with her.

Sally's suspicions about her inexplicable illness are aroused when she learns from Beatrice the details of

With Barbara Stanwyck

With Ann Carter

the first Mrs. Carroll's death. Her fears are substantiated when she goes to Geoffrey's studio and finds that she too has been painted as "The Angel of Death." Hounded by Blagdon, Geoffrey kills him and tells Cecily he is ready to go away with her. He sends Beatrice off to school in London, accompanied by Christine, the housekeeper.

He makes a final attempt to kill Sally with poisoned milk, but she throws it out a window while he is an-swering the phone and locks herself in ·her room. Finding traces of milk on the window ledge, Geoffrey realizes that Sally knows his intentions. He breaks in the window of her room and attempts to strangle her, thinking the crime will be blamed on a currently notorious strangler, but she thwarts him with a pistol borrowed from Charles Pennington, an old suitor. The police, summoned by Pennington after a desperate phone call from Sally, arrive and take Geoffrey away.

With Patrick O'Moore,
Barbara Stanwyck, and
Nigel Bruce

Dark Passage
1947

A Warner Bros.–First National Picture. Directed by Delmer Daves. Produced by Jerry Wald. Screenplay by Delmer Daves. Based on the novel by David Goodis. Director of photography, Sid Hickox. Music by Franz Waxman. Film editor, David Weisbart. Assistant director, Dick Mayberry. Art director, Charles H. Clarke. Set decorations by William Kuehl. Wardrobe by Bernard Newman. Makeup artist, Perc Westmore. Special effects by H. F. Koenekamp. Sound recorder, Dolph Thomas. Orchestrations by Leonid Raab. Running time, 106 minutes.

CAST

Vincent Parry	HUMPHREY BOGART
Irene Jansen	LAUREN BACALL
Bob Rapf	Bruce BENNETT
Madge Rapf	Agnes MOOREHEAD
Sam	Tom D'ANDREA
Baker	Clifton Young
Detective	Douglas Kennedy
George Fellsinger	Rory Mallinson
Dr. Walter Coley	Houseley Stevenson

With Lauren Bacall

With Lauren Bacall

With Agnes Moorehead

With Douglas Kennedy

SYNOPSIS

Vincent Parry escapes from San Quentin, where he has been imprisoned for slaying his wife. He is picked up by Irene Jansen, who smuggles him past a police roadblock. Irene, who has followed Parry's trial and believes him innocent, befriends him and takes him to her apartment. His safety is threatened when Irene is visited by Bob Rapf, who is courting her, and Bob's shrewish wife, Madge, who was a friend of Parry's wife and whose testimony convicted Parry.

Parry goes to a friend, George Fellsinger, for help in proving his innocence. Through Sam, a cab driver, Parry locates a plastic surgeon who alters his appearance. He returns to see George but finds him murdered. Going back to Irene, Parry remains in her apartment until his face heals. When the bandages are removed

Parry leaves, determined to clear himself and discover who killed his wife and Fellsinger.

In a cheap hotel room he is found by Baker, a petty crook who has recognized him and intends to blackmail him. They fight and Baker is accidentally killed, but not before he reveals that he saw Madge Rapf's car follow Parry to Fellsinger's. Parry goes to Madge's apartment and accuses her of killing both his wife and Fellsinger. Madge confesses, but robs Parry of his alibi when she accidentally falls to her death from a window.

With no hope of clearing himself, Parry tells Irene he must leave the country and, by now in love with her, asks her to join him. They meet in South America to start a new life together.

135

Always Together

1948

A Warner Bros.–First National Picture. Directed by Frederick de Cordova. Produced by Alex Gottlieb. Original screenplay by Phoebe & Henry Ephron and I. A. L. Diamond. Director of photography, Carl Guthrie. Music by Werner Heymann. Film editor, Folmer Blangsted. Dialogue director, John Maxwell. Assistant director, James McMahon. Art director, Leo K. Kuter. Set decorations by Jack McConaghy. Wardrobe by Travilla. Makeup artist, Perc Westmore. Special effects by William McGann and Edwin B. DuPar. Montages by James Leicester. Sound recorder, C. A. Riggs. Orchestrations by Leonid Raab. Running time, 78 minutes.

CAST

Donn Masters	ROBERT HUTTON
Jane Barker	JOYCE REYNOLDS
Jonathan Turner	Cecil KELLAWAY
Mr. Bull	Ernest TRUEX
McIntyre	Don McGuire
Judge	Ransom Sherman
Doberman	Douglas Kennedy

SYNOPSIS

Multimillionaire Jonathan Turner, on what he believes is his deathbed, leaves a million dollars to Jane Barker, a young secretary. Jane, a rabid movie addict who believes that life is just like it is in the movies, is engaged to Donn Masters, a struggling young writer. Having seen what happens in pictures when a rich girl tries to hold a poor but honest boy, Jane marries Donn without revealing the bequest.

Turner recovers, however, and wants his fortune back. He worms his way into the young couple's lives and tries to convince Jane that money isn't everything, but Donn learns of the gift and is elated at the prospect of living off the windfall. Finding her husband to be something less than the movie hero she imagined, Jane goes to Reno for a divorce, and Donn creates a national sensation by demanding alimony. They are reunited when it is disclosed that Turner's gift stemmed from his guilty conscience at having swindled Jane's father many years before.

In this picture a technique was used whereby "Jane" imagines personal experiences as if they were happening in motion pictures. Making unbilled appearances in these pictures-within-the-picture were Humphrey Bogart, Jack Carson, Errol Flynn, Dennis Morgan, Janis Paige, Eleanor Parker, and Alexis Smith.

Bogart's sequence, a take-off on *Stella Dallas*, drew this comment from *Time* magazine: "Best thing in the show: Humphrey Bogart—appearing briefly in a movie the girl goes to—as an outcast father, weeping against a rainy windowpane."

With John Huston

The Treasure

With Harry Vejar
and Tim Holt

With Tim Holt

of the Sierra Madre
1948

A Warner Bros.–First National Picture. Directed by John Huston. Produced by Henry Blanke. Screenplay by John Huston. Based on the novel by B. Traven. Director of photography, Ted McCord. Music by Max Steiner. Film editor, Owen Marks. Assistant director, Dick Mayberry. Art director, John Hughes. Set decorations by Fred M. MacLean. Makeup artist, Perc Westmore. Special effects by William McGann and H. F. Koenekamp. Sound recorder, Robert B. Lee. Orchestrations by Murray Cutter. Running time, 126 minutes.

CAST

Dobbs	HUMPHREY BOGART
Howard	WALTER HUSTON
Curtin	TIM HOLT
Cody	Bruce BENNETT
McCormick	Barton MacLane
Gold Hat	Alfonso Bedoya
Presidente	A. Soto Rangel
El Jefe	Manuel Donde
Pablo	Jose Torvay
Pancho	Margarito Luna
Flashy Girl	Jacqueline Dalya
Mexican Boy	Bobby Blake
White Suit	John Huston
Flophouse Bum	Jack Holt

With Tim Holt and
Barton MacLane

SYNOPSIS

Dobbs and Curtin, two Americans on the bum in Mexico, meet in the plaza in Tampico. Surfeited with cadging handouts, they take jobs in a construction camp, but their contractor, McCormick, decamps without paying them. In a flophouse they meet Howard, an old-time prospector, whose tales of gold-mining fire their imaginations. Encountering McCormick, they overcome him in a barroom fight and recover their earnings. With this money, and that won by Dobbs in a lottery, they have enough to buy provisions for a gold-hunting expedition. They seek out Howard, who agrees to accompany them, but warns them of the perils ahead and of the greed, distrust, and hatred that gold can cause.

En route to Durango, their train is ambushed by bandits whose leader is distinguished by his gold-colored hat. The attack is repelled by soldiers hidden aboard the train, and the three prospectors arrive in

With Bobby Blake

With Tim Holt, Jacqueline Dalya,
and Barton MacLane

With Tim Holt
and Walter Huston

138

Durango to buy burros and equipment for their expedition. Their trek into the mountainous Sierra Madre begins, and old Howard proves to be the hardiest of the three. As the tortuous trip proceeds, the first manifestations of bitterness appear, with Dobbs leading the bickering. They arrive at a site chosen by Howard and begin digging, eventually striking gold. Their find brings them tentative unity, and they work side by side to increase their riches, but as the gold dust accumulates friction returns. Dobbs becomes increasingly fearful and suspicious of his partners, and must be repeatedly cooled by Howard and Curtin as he falsely accuses them of coveting his "goods."

While in town for supplies, Curtin meets a Texan, Cody, who follows him to the camp and proposes partnership with the three miners. Egged on by the avaricious Dobbs, the partners decide that the interloper must be killed, but the execution is interrupted by the

With Walter Huston

With Tim Holt

With Tim Holt
and Walter Huston

With Tim Holt and Walter Huston

arrival of bandits, commanded by the same gold-hatted chieftain who led the attack on the train. After unsuccessfully attempting to obtain the prospectors' guns by barter, the bandits attack the camp, and during the battle Cody is killed. The bandits are routed by the sudden appearance of the *Federales*.

The three prospectors decide to call it a day and return to civilization. On the way down the mountain they are approached by friendly Indians, who tell of a boy near death from drowning. Howard accompanies them and revives the boy, and the grateful Indians make him a virtual prisoner as their village medicine man,

leaving Dobbs and Curtain to go on alone, Howard's share of the gold with them. The trip becomes a nightmare, as Dobbs' paranoia increases until, ridden by fear and distrust, he shoots Curtin. Leaving Curtin for dead, Dobbs continues on alone, with the burros and all the treasure in his possession. Curtin is found alive by Indians, who take him back to Howard.

As Dobbs pauses to drink from a waterhole, he is held up by three bandits, led by the familiar Gold Hat. When Dobbs resists them, they kill him and make off with his clothes and the burros, dashing the gold dust to the ground in the belief that it is dirt that was hidden

With Walter Huston and Bruce Bennett

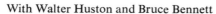

140

among the animal hides to make them weigh more and increase their value. In Durango the bandits attempt to sell the burros and hides, but are apprehended when the townspeople recognize Dobbs' clothing and identify the burros by their brand-marks. The bandits are swiftly executed just as Howard and Curtin ride into town. They hear of Dobbs' fate and rush to the scene, only to find themselves the victims of a cruel jest of fate. The desert winds have blown away their treasure, and they can only laugh at the sardonic end to their adventure.

John Huston won two Academy Awards for directing and writing *The Treasure of the Sierra Madre,* and Walter Huston captured a third as best supporting actor for his remarkable performance as "Howard." New York Film Critics Awards went to *Treasure* for best picture of the year and to John Huston for best direction.

With Alfonso Bedoya

Key Largo
1948

With Claire Trevor and Lauren Bacall

A Warner Bros.–First National Picture. Directed by John Huston. Produced by Jerry Wald. Screenplay by Richard Brooks and John Huston. Based on the play by Maxwell Anderson. Director of photography, Karl Freund. Music by Max Steiner. Film editor, Rudi Fehr. Assistant director, Art Lueker. Art director, Leo K. Kuter. Set decorations by Fred M. MacLean. Wardrobe by Leah Rhodes. Makeup artist, Perc Westmore. Special effects by William McGann and Robert Burks. Sound recorder, Dolph Thomas. Orchestrations by Murray Cutter. Song, "Moanin' Low," by Ralph Rainger and Howard Dietz. Running time, 101 minutes.

CAST

Frank McCloud	HUMPHREY BOGART
Johnny Rocco	EDWARD G. ROBINSON
Nora Temple	LAUREN BACALL
James Temple	Lionel BARRYMORE
Gaye Dawn	Claire TREVOR
Curley Hoff	Thomas Gomez
Toots Bass	Harry Lewis
Deputy Clyde Sawyer	John Rodney
Ziggy	Marc Lawrence
Angel Garcia	Dan Seymour
Sheriff Ben Wade	Monte Blue
Ralph Feeney	William Haade
Tom Osceola	Jay Silverheels
John Osceola	Rodric Redwing

With Lionel Barrymore and Lauren Bacall

With Harry Lewis, Dan Seymour, Edward G. Robinson, and Thomas Gomez

With Lauren Bacall

SYNOPSIS

Ex-Army major Frank McCloud, arriving on Key Largo, an island off the Florida coast, goes to a hotel run by James Temple and his daughter-in-law, Nora, the father and widow of a wartime comrade. McCloud finds the hotel taken over by a "Mr. Brown," his alcoholic girl friend, Gaye Dawn, and four henchmen, Curley, Toots, Angel, and Ralph. McCloud recognizes "Brown" as Johnny Rocco, a notorious deported racketeer, whom he views distastefully but apathetically. He rejects a chance to kill Rocco at the cost of his own life; he is disillusioned by the war's aftermath and is reluctant to fight again for any cause.

The island is swept by a storm, and Rocco becomes terrified, refusing to let Temple admit a group of Indians requesting shelter in the hotel. He promises Gaye

With Dan Seymour, Harry Lewis, and Lionel Barrymore

143

With Harry Lewis, Thomas Gomez,
and Dan Seymour

With Thomas Gomez,
Edward G. Robinson,
and Lauren Bacall

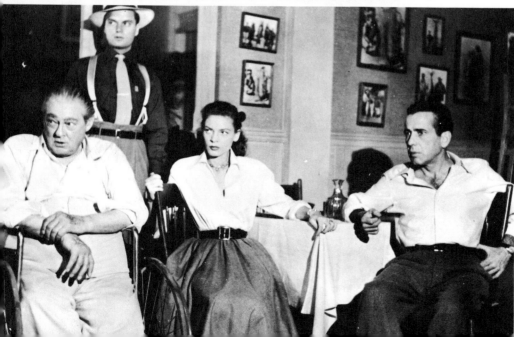

With Lionel Barrymore,
Harry Lewis,
and Lauren Bacall

With Thomas Gomez,
Edward G. Robinson,
and William Haade

a drink if she will sing an old favorite for him, but she is not the singer she once was, and her pathetic performance embarrasses them all. When Rocco cruelly refuses her the drink, McCloud pours it for her, taking a slapping from Rocco for his trouble. Nora and Temple ask McCloud to stay on at Key Largo and to look on them as his family.

When the storm abates, Rocco receives a visit from Ziggy, an old gangland crony who has come to buy a shipment of counterfeit money. After Ziggy departs, Sheriff Ben Wade comes looking for his deputy, Clyde Sawyer, who was after the Osceola brothers, two Indians on a drunken spree. When Wade finds the body of Sawyer, whom Rocco has killed, Rocco implies that the fugitive Osceolas are guilty. Wade finds the Indians and, when they try to get away, kills them both. Sick-

ened by Rocco's doings, McCloud realizes anew that there can be no compromise with evil, and he unexpectedly agrees to pilot a boat taking the gang to Cuba. When Rocco tells· Gaye that he is leaving her behind, she takes a gun from his pocket and passes it unseen to McCloud.

At sea, Rocco, Curley, and Angel go below, leaving Toots and Ralph on deck. Gunning the boat, McCloud throws Ralph overboard, shoots the seasick Toots, and picks off Curley as he comes up the passageway. Below, Rocco orders Angel topside, killing him when he refuses. Alone now, Rocco bargains with McCloud, offering him all the money obtained from Ziggy, but McCloud waits patiently for Rocco to show himself, and kills him when he does. Turning the boat around, McCloud heads back to Key Largo and the waiting Nora.

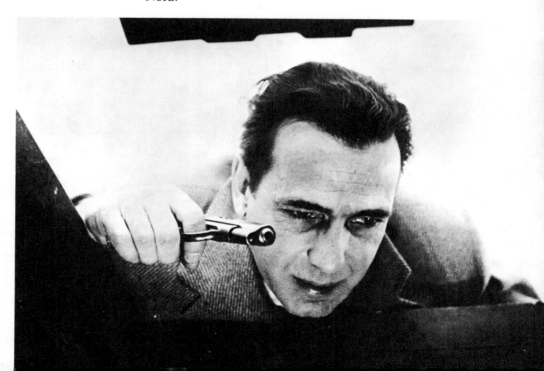

With John Derek

With Susan Perry

Knock on Any Door
1949

A Santana Production. Released by Columbia Pictures. Directed by Nicholas Ray. Produced by Robert Lord. Associate producer, Henry S. Kesler. Screenplay by Daniel Taradash and John Monks, Jr. Based on the novel by Willard Motley. Director of photography, Burnett Guffey. Music by George Antheil. Film editor, Viola Lawrence. Assistant director, Arthur S. Black. Art director, Robert Peterson. Set decorations by William Kiernan. Gowns by Jean Louis. Makeup artist, Clay Campbell. Hair styles by Helen Hunt. Sound recorder, Frank Goodwin. Orchestrations by Ernest Gold. Musical director, Morris Stoloff. Technical advisers, National Probation and Parole Association. Running time, 100 minutes.

With Dewey Martin and Robert A. Davis

With Barry Kelley and
Vince Barnett

CAST

Andrew Morton	HUMPHREY BOGART
Nick Romano	John DEREK
Kerman	George Macready
Emma	Allene Roberts
Adele Morton	Susan Perry
Vito	Mickey Knox
Judge Drake	Barry Kelley
Nelly	Cara Williams
Kid Fingers	Jimmy Conlin
Jimmy	Sumner Williams
Squint	Sid Melton
Juan	Pepe Hern
Butch	Dewey Martin
Sunshine	Robert A. Davis
Junior	Houseley Stevenson
Bartender	Vince Barnett
Officer Hawkins	Thomas Sully
Aunt Lena	Florence Auer
Purcell	Pierre Watkin
Corey	Gordon Nelson
Ma Romano	Argentina Brunetti
Julian Romano	Dick Sinatra
Ang Romano	Carol Coombs
Maria Romano	Joan Baxter

SYNOPSIS

Nick Romano, a slum-bred young hoodlum on trial for killing a policeman, is defended by attorney Andrew Morton, himself a successful graduate of the slums.

Nick's short history seemed to be made up of one petty crime after another. He even robbed Morton once, after Morton, at his wife Adele's insistence, tried to help Nick by taking him on a fishing trip. Then Nick married Emma, and he seemed to change for the better. He even took a job—several jobs, in fact—but he could never keep one. He was stunned when Emma told him she was pregnant; he had just squandered his pay check gambling, in an effort to buy her some jewelry. He returned to his old ways, but with a new motto: "Live fast, die young, and have a good-looking corpse." Returning from a holdup one night, he found Emma dead, a suicide by gas. Nearly insane with grief, Nick turned again to robbery, and when Officer Hawkins caught him, he pumped every bullet from his gun into the policeman's body.

But he brazens it out with Morton, telling him that he is innocent, and Morton nearly proves him so. District Attorney Kerman is unable to shake Nick's testimony and almost dismisses him from the witness stand

With John Derek

With Susan Perry

With George Macready (lower right) and John Derek (in dark coat)

when he suddenly thinks of another approach, almost absently, it seems. What, he asks, was the cause of Emma's death? Nick goes to pieces, and Kerman pounds in question after question until Nick shouts an admission of his guilt.

Morton, having believed Nick innocent, is stunned by his confession. In an eloquent appeal to the court, he notes that Nick also is guilty of seeing a young friend killed in a sadistic reform school, guilty of having to make his way without a father, guilty of living in one of the nation's worst slums. He argues that the slums are

breeding grounds for criminals, that if you knock on any door you may find a Nick Romano.

Nick is sentenced to die in the electric chair. Just before the execution, Morton visits Nick and watches as he walks the last mile.

In 1947 Bogart organized his own production company, Santana Pictures Corporation, with himself as president and producer Robert Lord as vice-president. *Knock on Any Door* was the first of four pictures starring Bogart which Santana made for Columbia Pictures.

Tokyo Joe
1949

A Santana Production. Released by Columbia Pictures. Directed by Stuart Heisler. Produced by Robert Lord. Associate producer, Henry S. Kesler. Screenplay by Cyril Hume and Bertram Millhauser. Adaptation by Walter Doniger. Based on a story by Steve Fisher. Director of photography, Charles Lawton, Jr. Music by George Antheil. Film editor, Viola Lawrence. Dialogue director, Jason Lindsey. Assistant director, Wilbur McGaugh. Art director, Robert Peterson. Set decorations by James Crowe. Gowns by Jean Louis. Makeup artist, Clay Campbell. Hair styles by Helen Hunt. Sound recorder, Russell Malmgren. Orchestrations by Ernest Gold. Musical director, Morris Stoloff. Running time, 88 minutes.

With Florence Marly

CAST

Joe Barrett	HUMPHREY BOGART
Mark Landis	Alexander KNOX
Trina	Florence MARLY
Baron Kimura	Sessue HAYAKAWA
Danny	Jerome Courtland
Idaho	Gordon Jones
Ito	Teru Shimada
Kanda	Hideo Mori
General Ireton	Charles Meredith
Colonel Dahlgren	Rhys Williams
Anya	Lora Lee Michael
Nani-San	Kyoko Kamo
Kamikaze	Gene Gondo
Major Loomis	Harold Goodwin
M. P. Captain	James Cardwell
Truck Driver	Frank Kumagai
Takenobu	Tetsu Komai
Hara	Otto Han
Goro	Yosan Tsuruta

With Florence Marly and Alexander Knox

With Sessue Hayakawa
and Teru Shimada

SYNOPSIS

After spending World War II in the Air Force, Joe Barrett returns to Tokyo, where before the war he owned a night club, Tokyo Joe's, and where he deserted his wife, Trina, in 1941. Finding Trina, he learns that she has divorced him and is now married to an American officer, Mark Landis. They have a seven-year-old daughter, Anya.

Through his ex-partner, Ito, Joe meets Baron Kimura, who offers to finance a small airline that will carry food delicacies for export. When Joe demurs, Kimura shows him proof that Trina made wartime propaganda broadcasts, a treasonable offense since she was married to an American citizen. When Joe faces Trina with this evidence, she explains that she made the broadcasts only

With Florence Marly
and Lora Lee Michael

With Hideo Mori

after the Japanese threatened to take her baby away from her. She reveals that Anya is Joe's daughter, that she was pregnant when he deserted her.

To save Trina, Joe accepts Kimura's proposal, but he soon finds that besides carrying freight, he is to smuggle three Japanese war criminals back into Japan. He notifies American occupation authorities, who plan to apprehend the Japanese as they land. But as Joe is about to leave on the mission, Kimura informs him that Anya has been kidnapped and will be killed unless the Japanese are delivered by a certain deadline. Joe picks up his passengers and is about to land them at an Army-designated airfield when the Japanese produce guns and land the plane at another airstrip. However, military police are waiting there, too, and the Japanese are taken into custody.

With only an hour left before the deadline, Joe learns from Ito that Anya is being held in a nearby cavern. He enters the dark cave and finds Anya, but he is shot by Kimura as he carries the little girl to safety. Kimura is killed by arriving American soldiers, but Joe, having saved his child's life, pays with his own.

With Lora Lee Michael

Chain Lightning
1950

With Eleanor Parker

A Warner Bros.–First National Picture. Directed by Stuart Heisler. Produced by Anthony Veiller. Screenplay by Liam O'Brien and Vincent Evans. Based on an original story by J. Redmond Prior. Director of photography, Ernest Haller. Music by David Buttolph. Film editor, Thomas Reilly. Assistant director, Don Page. Art director, Leo K. Kuter. Set decorations by William Wallace. Gowns by Leah Rhodes. Makeup artist, Perc Westmore. Special effects by William McGann, Harry Barndollar, H. F. Koenekamp and Edwin B. DuPar. Sound recorder, Francis J. Scheid. Orchestrations by Maurice de Packh. Song, "Bless 'Em All," by J. Hughes, Frank Lake, and Al Stillman. Running time, 94 minutes.

With Richard Whorf, James Brown, Eleanor Parker, and Jack Reynolds

With Eleanor Parker and Morris Ankrum

CAST

Matt Brennan	HUMPHREY BOGART
Jo Holloway	ELEANOR PARKER
Leland Willis	Raymond MASSEY
Carl Troxell	Richard WHORF
Major Hinkle	James BROWN
General Hewitt	Roy Roberts
Ed Bostwick	Morris Ankrum
Mrs. Willis	Fay Baker
Jeb Farley	Fred Sherman

SYNOPSIS

In 1943 Matt Brennan is completing a tour of duty over Europe as a bomber pilot. His romance with Jo Holloway, a Red Cross girl, is interrupted when he is ordered home after his twenty-fifth mission.

After the war, as Matt works as a barnstorming pilot, a wartime buddy, Major Hinkle, takes him to a party given by Leland Willis, a jet plane manufacturer. Here Matt again meets Jo, now Willis' secretary, and renews his romance with her. Willis hires him as a test pilot for a new jet that Willis hopes to sell to the Air Force. Carl Troxell, Willis' designer, asks Matt not to report the plane ready for flight until he perfects a new escape-cockpit, but Willis, eager for Air Force approval, offers Matt $30,000 to pilot the unsafe jet over the pole from Nome to Washington, D.C., in a publicity bid for the Air Force contract.

The flight is successful, but Carl, attempting to offset Matt's publicity, rushes his work and is killed testing his safety device. Blaming himself and blamed by Jo for Carl's death, Matt, using information left by Carl, flies a jet equipped with the escape device for the final Air Force tests. Ejecting himself in Carl's escape cockpit, he lands safely. The Air Force gets the safe plane and Matt gets Jo.

With Eleanor Parker and
Richard Whorf

With Martha Stewart

In a Lonely Place
1950

A Santana Production. Released by Columbia Pictures. Directed by Nicholas Ray. Produced by Robert Lord. Associate producer, Henry S. Kesler. Screenplay by Andrew Solt. Adaptation by Edmund H. North. Based on the novel by Dorothy B. Hughes. Director of photography, Burnett Guffey. Music by George Antheil. Film editor, Viola Lawrence. Assistant director, Earl Bellamy. Art director, Robert Peterson. Set decorations by William Kiernan. Gowns by Jean Louis. Makeup artist, Clay Campbell. Hair styles by Helen Hunt. Sound recorder, Howard Fogetti. Orchestrations by Ernest Gold. Musical director, Morris Stoloff. Technical adviser, Rodney Amateau. Running time, 94 minutes.

CAST

Dixon Steele	HUMPHREY BOGART
Laurel Gray	Gloria GRAHAME
Brub Nicolai	Frank Lovejoy
Captain Lochner	Carl Benton Reid
Mel Lippman	Art Smith
Sylvia Nicolai	Jeff Donnell
Mildred Atkinson	Martha Stewart
Charlie Waterman	Robert Warwick
Lloyd Barnes	Morris Ankrum
Ted Barton	William Ching
Paul	Steven Geray
Singer	Hadda Brooks
Frances Randolph	Alice Talton
Henry Kesler	Jack Reynolds
Effie	Ruth Warren
Martha	Ruth Gillette
Swan	Guy Beach
Junior	Lewis Howard

With Art Smith and Gloria Grahame

154

With Gloria Grahame

With Frank Lovejoy,
Carl Benton Reid,
and Gloria Grahame

SYNOPSIS

Screenwriter Dixon Steele undertakes the scripting of a trashy novel but can't face reading it. He induces Mildred Atkinson, a hat-check girl who has read the book, to come to his apartment and tell him the story. Later Mildred is found murdered and Dix is suspected, but he is released after a neighbor, Laurel Gray, testifies that she was watching from her balcony as Dix sent Mildred home in a cab.

Dix begins to write furiously on the screenplay, and Laurel all but moves in with him, typing the manuscript,

seeing to meals, banishing intruders. Mel Lippman, Dix's agent, is delighted, for Dix is working well for the first time in years, and Laurel is the reason. But the Atkinson case is unsolved; still suspected are Mildred's boy friend—whom she stood up in order to read to Dix —and Dix himself. Brub Nicolai, the detective on the case and a wartime friend of Dix's, tells Laurel of Dix's notorious proclivity for violence, and Laurel shortly witnesses this penchant at first hand. She is driving home with Dix after a beach party with the Nicolais,

155

With Art Smith, Robert Warwick, and Gloria Grahame

when he collides with a boy in a jalopy. Dix beats the youth unconscious, although later he sends the boy an anonymous money order.

Alarmed, Laurel consults Sylvia, who advises her to leave Dix, and even Mel agrees that she must flee if she fears Dix. But the writing goes on, the typing goes on, and Laurel finally is trapped into a decision when Dix proposes. She says Yes, even though the unsolved murder, the uncertain alibi, and Dix's tendencies toward violence have driven her to sleeping pills.

At a celebration dinner at Paul's restaurant, Dix learns that Mel has taken his unfinished script. Dix hits him, the party disintegrates, and Laurel leaves. Dix pursues her home and is asking forgiveness when a phone call from a plane agency, which he intercepts, confirms a reservation for Laurel. Angered beyond control, he begins choking her when the phone rings again. It is the police, calling to say that Mildred's boy friend has confessed her murder. But it is too late; they both know that everything between them is over. Dix walks out without looking back, and Laurel goes to the window to watch him cross the patio and go out of her life.

With Gloria Grahame

With Roy Roberts and Zero Mostel

The Enforcer
1951

A United States Picture for Warner Bros. Directed by Bretaigne Windust. Produced by Milton Sperling. Original screenplay by Martin Rackin. Director of photography, Robert Burks. Music by David Buttolph. Film editor, Fred Allen. Assistant director, Chuck Hansen. Art director, Charles H. Clarke. Set decorations by William Kuehl. Sound recorder, Dolph Thomas. Orchestrations by Maurice de Packh. Running time, 87 minutes.

With Roy Roberts

CAST

Martin Ferguson	HUMPHREY BOGART
Big Babe Lazich	Zero Mostel
Joseph Rico	Ted De Corsia
Albert Mendoza	Everett Sloane
Capt. Frank Nelson	Roy Roberts
Duke Malloy	Lawrence Tolan
Sgt. Whitlow	King Donovan
Herman	Bob Steele
Olga Kirshen	Adelaide Klein
Thomas O'Hara	Don Beddoe
Tony Vetto	Tito Vuolo
Vince	John Kellogg
Philadelphia Tom Zaca	Jack Lambert
Angela Vetto	Patricia Joiner
Nina Lombardo	Susan Cabot
Louis the Barber	Mario Siletti

SYNOPSIS

After years of effort, Assistant District Attorney Martin Ferguson has built a case against Albert Mendoza, head of Murder, Inc. The police have arrested Joseph Rico, Mendoza's lieutenant and a witness to a murder Mendoza once committed. Although Mendoza himself is in jail awaiting trial, Rico, fearful that he will be killed before he can testify, attempts to escape and falls to his death. Determined to glean some clue from the mass of records on the Mendoza case, Ferguson works through the night reviewing the files.

The case started when Duke Malloy surrendered to

With Roy Roberts and King Donovan

With Roy Roberts (right)

the police and confessed that he killed Nina Lombardo because she was a "hit" and he had the "contract." Ferguson questioned Nina's roommate, Teresa Davis, but Teresa knew nothing of Nina's past except that she once admitted her real name was Angela Vetto. Duke's testimony led Ferguson to one gang member after another, and eventually more than a score of the gang's victims were found buried in a swamp. The press was given the story and the heat was on.

Rico phoned Ferguson to arrange a deal: in return for clemency he would testify against Mendoza. He told Ferguson of first meeting Mendoza in a cafe, where Mendoza had outlined his plan to sell murder as a commodity. Mendoza had argued that when the killer had no motive, the police had no chance of learning the killer's identity. To illustrate his point, Mendoza had calmly killed the café owner. However, Rico and Mendoza had been seen leaving by two witnesses, Tony Vetto and his daughter, Angela. Years later Mendoza had come upon Vetto and had had him killed. His daughter, who had moved to another city and changed her name, was traced too, and killed by Duke Malloy.

As Ferguson listens to a recording of Rico's testimony he suddenly gets the clue he needs. Rico refers to Vetto's daughter as having blue eyes, but the dead girl, Nina Lombardo, had brown eyes. Ferguson realizes that Nina was mistaken for Angela Vetto and that Nina's roommate, Teresa Davis, is the real Angela. Learning that a hired gunman, Herman, is after Angela, Ferguson reaches her just in time. As Herman tries to shoot Angela, Ferguson guns him down, saving the one witness who can send Mendoza to the chair.

With Ted DeCorsia

Sirocco

1951

A Santana Production. Released by Columbia Pictures. Directed by Curtis Bernhardt. Produced by Robert Lord. Associate producer, Henry S. Kesler. Screenplay by A. I. Bezzerides and Hans Jacoby. Based on the novel Coup de Grâce *by Joseph Kessel. Director of photography, Burnett Guffey. Music by George Antheil. Film editor, Viola Lawrence. Assistant director, Earl Bellamy. Art director, Robert Peterson. Set decorations by Robert Priestley. Makeup artist, Clay Campbell. Hair styles by Helen Hunt. Sound recorder, Lodge Cunningham. Orchestrations by Ernest Gold. Musical director, Morris Stoloff. Running time, 98 minutes.*

CAST

Harry Smith	HUMPHREY BOGART
Violette	Marta TOREN
Colonel Feroud	Lee J. COBB
General LaSalle	Everett Sloane
Major Leon	Gerald Mohr
Balukjian	Zero Mostel
Nasir Aboud	Nick Dennis
Emir Hassan	Onslow Stevens
Flophouse Proprietor	Ludwig Donath
Achmet	David Bond
Arthur	Vincent Renno
Omar	Martin Wilkins
Major Robbinet	Peter Ortiz
Colonel Corville	Edward Colmans
Sergeant	Al Eben
Barber	Peter Brocco
Hamal	Jay Novello
Rifat	Leonard Penn
Lieutenant Collet	Harry Guardino

With Lee J. Cobb

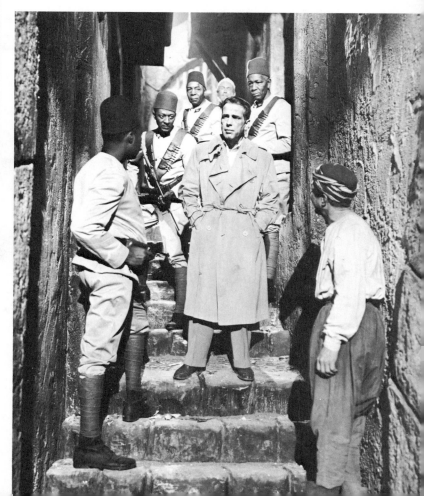

In 1925, in French-occupied Damascus, Harry Smith plies a profitable trade running guns to the rebel army of the Emir Hassan. Colonel Feroud, head of French Intelligence, sends Lieutenant Collet to Hassan on a peace mission, and rounds up a group of suspects, including Harry, compelling them to sell their guns to the French. Harry complies, but gains partial revenge by making successful overtures to Feroud's mistress, Violette. Telling Feroud she is through with him, Violette requests a pass to Cairo, but Feroud refuses.

In the catacombs under Damascus, Harry collects his last payment from the Syrians. He has been informed on and is no longer useful, and Hassan warns him never to enter the catacombs again. Harry attempts to leave Damascus with Violette, but Feroud's police thwart their departure at the bus depot. Harry escapes and Violette is arrested, but Feroud, still in love with her, merely sends her back to her apartment.

Collet's body is returned by the Syrians, and Feroud determines to seek a truce with Hassan himself, without permission from General LaSalle. Feroud offers Harry a pass to Cairo in exchange for arranging a meeting with Hassan, and Harry agrees, turning Feroud over to Hassan's emissary. Applying for his pass, Harry is ushered before General LaSalle, who tries to persuade him to help the French rescue Feroud. When Harry refuses, LaSalle gives him the pass anyway, along with one for Violette that Feroud had generously provided before going to his almost certain death. Something about the act breaks Harry down, and he tells LaSalle that he thinks he can buy Feroud's release, as the Syrians need money badly.

Harry takes the ransom money to the forbidden catacombs, where Feroud's proposals are being ridiculed by Hassan. Treating the situation as a grim joke, Hassan accepts the ransom and releases Feroud, admiring him for his bravery, but orders Harry, the man who works only for money, killed with a hand grenade.

With Marta Toren

With Marta Toren

160

The African Queen
1951

A Horizon-Romulus Production. Released thru United Artists. Color by Technicolor. Directed by John Huston. Produced by S. P. Eagle (Sam Spiegel). Screenplay by James Agee and John Huston. Based on the novel by C. S. Forester. Director of photography, Jack Cardiff. Music by Alan Gray, played by the Royal Philharmonic Orchestra conducted by Norman Del Mar. Film editor, Ralph Kemplen. Assistant director, Guy Hamilton. Art director, Wilfred Shingleton; associate, John Hoesli. Production managers, Leigh Aman and T. S. Lyndon-Haynes. Miss Hepburn's costumes by Doris Langley Moore; other clothes by Connie De Pinna. Makeup artist, George Frost. Second unit photography by Ted Scaife. Special effects by Cliff Richardson. Sound recorder, John Mitchell. Sound editor, Eric Wood. Camera operator, Ted Moore. Hairdresser, Eileen Bates. Wardrobe mistress, Vi Murray. Continuity by Angela Allen. Running time, 105 minutes.

CAST

Charlie Allnut	HUMPHREY BOGART
Rose Sayer	KATHARINE HEPBURN
Rev. Samuel Sayer	Robert MORLEY
Captain of the *Louisa*	Peter Bull
First Officer (*Louisa*)	Theodore Bikel
Second Officer (*Louisa*)	Walter Gotell
Petty Officer (*Louisa*)	Gerald Onn
First Officer (*Shona*)	Peter Swanwick
Second Officer (*Shona*)	Richard Marner

With Katharine Hepburn

With Katharine Hepburn

SYNOPSIS

At the outbreak of World War I, German troops set fire to a Central African village and drive off the natives. The shock kills the village missionary, Reverend Samuel Sayer, leaving his sister Rose alone. She is taken aboard the *African Queen,* a squat, 30-foot river launch, by its dissolute Canadian skipper, Charlie Allnut. Allnut has plenty of cigarettes and gin, and favors sitting out the war in some backwater, but Rose conceives a daring plan to take the *African Queen* down the river to a lake and there destroy a German gunboat that commands the only invasion route open to British forces. Allnut is skeptical, but Rose is so adamant that he reluctantly pushes off, with her as his passenger.

As they run the first rapids, Rose experiences the first real excitement of her life, but Allnut refuses to go on and proceeds to get drunk. He awakes the next morning to find Rose pouring all his gin overboard, but she converts his ensuing rage to shame and they head downriver again. Taking the *African Queen* through gunfire from a German fort and over perilous rapids, they eventually reach a peaceful cove, where, in the emotional relief of their triumph, they fall into each other's arms.

Surviving malaria, insects, and leeches, and cataracts that damage the boat and force them ashore for a week of repairs, they finally arrive at the lake where the German gunboat, the *Louisa,* sails unchallenged. Allnut fashions two torpedos from oxygen cylinders and blasting gelatine and attaches them to the *African Queen,* intending to ram the enemy. As they set out for their target, the *African Queen* is swamped in a storm, and

With Katharine Hepburn

With Katharine Hepburn

With Katharine Hepburn

With Katharine Hepburn

Allnut and Rose are taken aboard the *Louisa* and sentenced to be hanged as enemy agents. Allnut asks the Captain to marry them before they die, but just as the ceremony ends the *Louisa* runs into the derelict *African Queen* and blows up. Thrown into the water, Allnut and Rose merrily paddle off toward the shore.

For his performance as "Charlie Allnut," Bogart won the Academy Award for Best Actor of 1951. He had been considered a dark horse contestant, and early straw polls favored Marlon Brando for *A Streetcar Named Desire*. Indeed, Brando's co-stars won three out of the four acting awards—Best Actress (Vivien Leigh), Best Supporting Actress (Kim Hunter), and Best Supporting Actor (Karl Malden).

But Bogart was the popular choice, and the announcement of his name brought the house down as he loped on stage to receive his Oscar from Greer Garson. Looking as surprised as everyone else, Bogey panted: "It's a long way from the Belgian Congo to the stage of the Pantages, but it's a lot nicer here. I want to pay tribute to John Huston and Katharine Hepburn, who helped me to be where I am now."

Considering the caliber of some of his previous performances, many found it hard to believe that *The African Queen* alone was responsible for his victory and that sentiment played no part in his selection. Perhaps Bogart summed it up best himself: "I've been around a long time. Maybe the people like me."

With Theodore Bikel

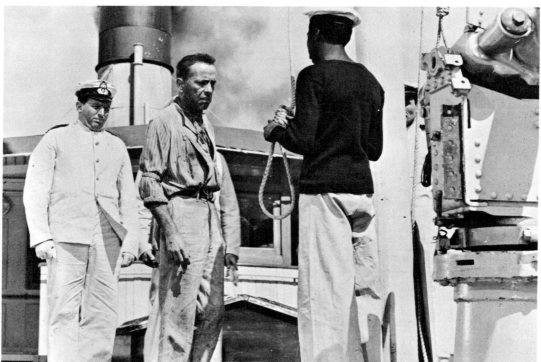

164

Deadline–U.S.A.
1950

With Ethel Barrymore

A 20th Century–Fox Picture. Directed by Richard Brooks. Produced by Sol C. Siegel. Original screenplay by Richard Brooks. Director of photography, Milton Krasner. Music by Cyril Mockridge and Sol Kaplan. Film editor, William B. Murphy. Assistant director, Dick Mayberry. Art directors, Lyle Wheeler and George Patrick. Set decorations by Thomas Little and Walter M. Scott. Wardrobe direction, Charles Le Maire. Costumes by Eloise Jenssen. Makeup artist, Ben Nye. Special effects by Ray Kellogg. Sound recorders, E. Clayton Ward and Harry M. Leonard. Orchestrations by Edward Powell and Bernard Mayers. Musical director, Lionel Newman. Running time, 87 minutes.

CAST

Ed Hutchinson	HUMPHREY BOGART
Mrs. Garrison	Ethel BARRYMORE
Nora	Kim HUNTER
Frank Allen	Ed Begley
George Burrows	Warren Stevens
Harry Thompson	Paul Stewart
Tomas Rienzi	Martin Gabel
Herman Schmidt	Joe De Santis
Kitty Garrison Geary	Joyce MacKenzie
Mrs. Willebrandt	Audrey Christie
Alice Garrison Courtney	Fay Baker
Jim Cleary	Jim Backus
Crane	Carleton Young
Williams	Selmer Jackson
Judge	Fay Roope
Headwaiter	Parley Baer
Hal	John Douchette
Miss Barndollar	Florence Shirley
Mrs. Schmidt	Kasia Orzazewski
Lawrence White	Raymond Greenleaf
Wharton	Tom Powers
Fenway	Thomas Browne Henry
Lewis Schaefer	Philip Terry
Whitey	Joseph Sawyer
Larry Hansen	Lawrence Dobkin
Prentiss	Alex Gerry
Captain Finlay	Clancy Cooper
Henry	Willis Bouchey
White's City Editor	Joseph Crehan

With Kim Hunter

With Ed Begley, Joe DeSantis
and Paul Stewart

With Kim Hunter

SYNOPSIS

After a Senate probe into the activities of alleged vice king Tomas Rienzi proves fruitless, George Burrows, a reporter for *The Day,* asks to be kept on the story, certain that he can uncover proof of Rienzi's criminal involvements. Burrows' managing editor, Ed Hutchinson, gives his approval, but his real concern is another story—that *The Day* is to be sold. Hutchinson is summoned to a meeting of *The Day's* owners, Mrs. John Garrison, widow of the paper's founder, and her daughters, Alice Garrison Courtney and Kitty Garrison Geary, who are selling *The Day* to Lawrence White, owner of the rival *Standard*. The paper will be published for two more days, until the Surrogate Court approves the sale.

After getting tight at a wake for the beloved paper, Hutchinson visits his divorced wife, Nora, and suggests that they remarry, but Nora reveals her engagement to another man. The next morning Hutchinson learns that Burrows has been badly beaten by Rienzi's thugs, and

that a girl whose body was found in the river the day before has been identified as Bessie Schmidt. Herman Schmidt, Bessie's brother, is found, and admits that his sister was killed by Rienzi's men because she refused to return $200,000 which she was holding for Rienzi. But before Schmidt can sign his statement, he is taken away by two Rienzi gunmen dressed as policemen and killed.

The Surrogate Court approves the sale of *The Day*, with legal ownership to be transferred the next day. As Hutchinson is confirming the sale to Frank Allen, his city editor, Allen tells him to return to the office immediately. There Hutchinson finds Mrs. Schmidt, with not only the $200,000 but also Bessie's diary, which incriminates Rienzi on nearly every page. While Hutchinson is preparing the story for publication, Nora enters his office; she has come back to him for good. As press time approaches, Rienzi calls Hutchinson, warning him not to print the story, but the only reply he hears is a great roar, as *The Day's* courageous final edition goes to press.

U.S. Savings Bonds trailer

1952

Bogart presented the Series E Savings Bonds in a special trailer made by Metro-Goldwyn-Mayer and attached to the July 25-26 newsreel releases.

With Robert Keith and June Allyson

With Perry Sheehan and William Campbell

Battle Circus
1953

A Metro-Goldwyn-Mayer Picture. Directed by Richard Brooks. Produced by Pandro S. Berman. Screenplay by Richard Brooks. Based on an original story by Allen Rivkin and Laura Kerr. Director of photography, John Alton. Music by Lennie Hayton. Film editor, George Boemler. Assistant director, Al Jennings. Art directors, Cedric Gibbons and James Basevi. Set decorations by Edwin B. Willis and Alfred E. Spencer. Makeup artist, William Tuttle. Special effects by A. Arnold Gillespie. Recording supervisor, Douglas Shearer. Orchestrations by Robert Franklyn. Technical advisers, Lt. Col. K. E. Van Buskirk and Lt. Mary Couch. Running time, 90 minutes.

CAST

Major Jed Webbe	HUMPHREY BOGART
Lt. Ruth McCara	JUNE ALLYSON
Sgt. Orvil Statt	Keenan WYNN
Lt. Col. Hillary Whalters	Robert KEITH
Capt. John Rustford	William Campbell
Lt. Laurence	Perry Sheehan
Lt. Rose Ashland	Patricia Tiernan
Adjutant	Jonathan Cott
Lt. Jane Franklin	Adele Longmire
Lt. Edith Edwards	Ann Morrison
Lt. Graciano	Helen Winston
Capt. Dobbs	Sarah Selby
Danny	Danny Chang
Korean Prisoner	Philip Ahn
Sergeant	Steve Forrest
Lieutenant	Jeff Richards
Capt. Norson	Dick Simmons

With June Allyson

With William Campbell

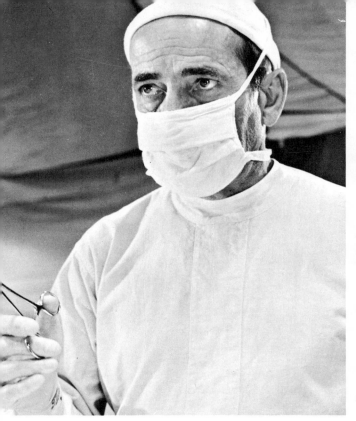

With June Allyson

Synopsis

A group of Army relief nurses arrives at Major Jed Webbe's mobile field hospital behind the front lines in Korea. Among them is Lt. Ruth McCara, all a-thrill over the prospect of serving suffering humanity. She catches Webbe's attention immediately because of the unnecessary risks she takes, and he starts a succession of passes to relieve the grimness of his medical chores. Webbe participates in a helicopter pickup of front-line casualties while under fire, and is harassed by the continual moving necessitated by the changing battle lines. In charge of disassembling and repitching the temporary tent hospital is Sgt. Orvil Statt, a former circus roustabout.

Under Webbe's tutelage, Ruth begins to shape up, and she proves her courage by disarming a battle-crazed Korean prisoner who threatens his captors with a hand grenade. No less perilous is her intermittent romance with Webbe, whose weakness for women is equalled by his opposition to wedlock. Webbe also has a weakness for liquor under stress: "Three world wars in one lifetime. Maybe whisky's as much a part of our life as war." But he tapers off after Colonel Whalters threatens him with transfer if he doesn't stop drinking. Webbe's antipathy to marriage almost causes a rift between the lovers, but after a separation dictated by military needs they are reunited.

With Keenan Wynn

169

With Jennifer Jones and Gina Lollobrigida

Beat the Devil
1954

With Gina Lollobrigida
and Edward Underdown

With Gina Lollobrigida,
Edward Underdown, Alex Pochet,
and Jennifer Jones

With Jennifer Jones

A Santana-Romulus Production. Released thru United Artists. Directed by John Huston. Associate producer, Jack Clayton. Screenplay by John Huston and Truman Capote. Based on the novel by James Helvick. Director of photography, Oswald Morris. Music by Franco Mannino. Film editor, Ralph Kemplen. Art director, Wilfred Shingleton. Sound recorders, George Stephenson and E. Law. Musical director, Lambert Williamson. Running time, 93 minutes.

CAST

Billy Dannreuther	HUMPHREY BOGART
Gwendolen Chelm	JENNIFER JONES
Maria Dannreuther	GINA LOLLOBRIGIDA
Petersen	Robert MORLEY
O'Hara	Peter LORRE
Harry Chelm	Edward UNDERDOWN
Major Ross	Ivor Barnard
C.I.D. Inspector	Bernard Lee
Ravello	Marco Tulli
Purser	Mario Perroni
Hotel Manager	Alex Pochet
Charles	Aldo Silvani
Administrator	Guilio Donnini
Captain	Saro Urzi
Hispano-Suiza Driver	Juan de Landa
Arab Officer	Manuel Serano
Barman	Mimo Poli

SYNOPSIS

Six adventurers are stranded at a small Italian port while their steamer is being repaired. One group is a quartet of international crooks—Petersen, O'Hara, Ross, and Ravello. The other consists of their frontman, an American fortune hunter named Billy Dannreuther, and his wife, Maria, who pass the four scoundrels off as their "business associates." They are bound for British East Africa, ostensibly to sell vacuum cleaners in Kenya, but actually to buy up some public land on a private tip that the place is loaded with uranium. With a passion for secrecy, the four conspirators see danger everywhere, having already murdered one potential blabber in London.

While waiting for passage, Billy and Maria take up

With Gina Lollobrigida, Peter Lorre, Robert Morley, Jennifer Jones, and Marco Tulli

171

With Robert Morley,
Ivor Barnard, Peter Lorre,
Marco Tulli, Jennifer Jones,
and Gina Lollobrigida

with another couple, Harry and Gwendolen Chelm. Harry is a dimwitted bogus British peer, his wife an inveterate liar. Overhearing Gwendolen's imaginative babblings about uranium holdings, the plotters are convinced that their project is in danger of a double-cross. Billy starts to hustle Gwendolen, believing from her talk that her husband can lead him to uranium, while Maria makes overtures of her own to Harry. The four villains watch this amatory game with alarm, reading into it a counterplot to deactivate the uranium deal.

Their ship is finally repaired, and they push off for Africa. Harry tumbles to the quartet's scheme, and they try to murder him; when he denounces them, they have him put in irons as a paranoiac. The steamer opportunely blows up and starts to sink, and Harry disappears overboard. The seven survivors manage to reach land in a lifeboat, only to be fired upon by Arab police because they have come ashore illegally. Seized as spies, they are interrogated by an Arab officer whose goal in life is to meet Rita Hayworth, and are released only after Billy promises the officer an interview with the object of his admiration.

Back in Italy, the four cutthroats are rounded up by the law after Gwendolen, for once in her life, tells the truth. She receives a telegram from her presumably drowned husband asking her to come back—all is forgiven. She bids a tearful farewell to Billy and Maria, who read the telegram, find that Harry has acquired the uranium land for himself.

With Peter Lorre, Robert Morley,
Marco Tulli, Gina Lollobrigida,
and Jennifer Jones

The Caine Mutiny
1954

A Stanley Kramer Company Production. Released by Columbia Pictures. Color by Technicolor. Directed by Edward Dmytryk. Produced by Stanley Kramer. Screenplay by Stanley Roberts. Additional dialogue by Michael Blankfort. Based on the novel by Herman Wouk. Director of photography, Franz Planer. Music by Max Steiner. Production design by Rudolph Sternad. Film editors, William Lyon and Henry Batista. Assistant director, Carter DeHaven, Jr. Art director, Cary Odell. Set decorations by Frank Tuttle. Gowns by Jean Louis. Makeup artist, Clay Campbell. Hair styles by Helen Hunt. Second unit photography by Ray Cory. Special effects by Lawrence Butler. Sound recorder, Lambert Day. Songs: "I Can't Believe That You're in Love With Me" by Jimmy McHugh and Clarence Gaskill; "Yellowstain Blues" by Fred Karger and Herman Wouk. Color consultant, Francis Cugat. Technical adviser, Comdr. James C. Shaw, U.S.N. Running time, 125 minutes.

With Tom Tully, Jerry Paris, Fred MacMurray,
Arthur Franz, Robert Francis, and Van Johnson

CAST

Captain Queeg	HUMPHREY BOGART
Lt. Barney Greenwald	JOSE FERRER
Lt. Steve Maryk	VAN JOHNSON
Lt. Tom Keefer	FRED MACMURRAY
Ensign Willie Keith	Robert FRANCIS
May Wynn	May WYNN
Captain DeVriess	Tom Tully
Lt. Comdr. Challee	E. G. Marshall
Lt. Paynter	Arthur Franz
Meatball	Lee Marvin
Captain Blakely	Warner Anderson
Horrible	Claude Akins
Mrs. Keith	Katharine Warren
Ensign Harding	Jerry Paris
Chief Budge	Steve Brodie
Stilwell	Todd Karns
Lt. Comdr. Dickson	Whit Bissell
Lt. Jorgensen	James Best
Ensign Carmody	Joe Haworth
Ensign Rabbit	Guy Anderson
Whittaker	James Edwards
Urban	Don Dubbins
Engstrand	David Alpert

SYNOPSIS

In 1943, Ensign Willie Keith is assigned to the destroyer *Caine* at Pearl Harbor, where he meets Lieutenant Maryk, the executive officer, and Lieutenant Keefer, a peacetime novelist. Shocked at the general disorder of the ship, Willie is pleased when Captain DeVriess is replaced—by Lieutenant Commander Philip Francis Queeg. But Queeg is no ordinary spit-and-polish officer. While the *Caine* is engaged in target-towing practice, Queeg becomes so involved in berating an unkempt sailor that he allows the ship to steam in a circle and cut its own towline.

Later, while leading Marine landing craft toward an island beachhead, Queeg moves the *Caine* in too fast and finds himself under shore fire. Rather than wait for the attack boats to catch up, Queeg orders a yellow-dye marker thrown onto the water at the point he is to leave them, and gets the ship out of range as fast as possible. As a result of Queeg's apparent cowardice, the men call him Old Yellowstain, and even make up a song, the "Yellowstain Blues." In a roundabout way Queeg asks for the sympathy and understanding of his officers, but his request is met with silence. Keefer suggests that Queeg is paranoid, and so influences Maryk that he secretly begins keeping a medical log on Queeg.

Other incidents follow indicating Queeg's unbalance, culminating in Queeg's discovery that some strawberries are missing from the wardroom icebox. Although told that they were eaten by the messboys, Queeg insists they were stolen and conducts a shipboard search for an imaginary duplicate icebox key. Admitting that Keefer's estimation of Queeg may be correct, Maryk goes to see Admiral Halsey aboard his aircraft carrier, but Keefer gets cold feet and persuades Maryk to back out.

During a typhoon, in which the *Caine* seems in danger of foundering, Maryk invokes a Navy article providing for the relief of a captain by his executive officer under certain emergency conditions. Willie supports Maryk, and Queeg threatens them with charges of mutiny.

Back in San Francisco, Maryk is brought before a court-martial, where he is defended by Lieutenant Barney Greenwald. The prosecution, Lieutenant Commander Challee, martials much evidence as to Queeg's experience and ability, and even Keefer reverses his position, putting sole blame on Maryk. When Queeg takes the stand, however, he hedges and becomes confused, and under Greenwald's incisive questioning is

With Van Johnson and Todd Karns

finally reduced to a pathetic, babbling ruin. Maryk and Willie are acquitted.

As the *Caine's* officers hold a celebration, Greenwald enters and rebukes them for what they did to Queeg, who was protecting the country long before they entered the wartime Navy. Toasting "the real author of the *Caine* mutiny," Greenwald dashes his champagne in Keefer's face.

Assigned to a new ship, Willie finds it commanded by Captain DeVriess, the original captain of the *Caine*.

The role of "Captain Queeg" brought Bogart his third Academy nomination. The award went to Marlon Brando for *On the Waterfront*.

With E. G. Marshall (third from left) Robert Bray, Paul McGuire, Kenneth MacDonald, Warner Anderson, Tyler McVey, Gaylord Pendleton, Van Johnson, and Jose Ferrer.

With Audrey Hepburn

With Audrey Hepburn and William Holden

Sabrina
1954

A Paramount Picture. Produced and directed by Billy Wilder. Screenplay by Billy Wilder, Samuel Taylor, and Ernest Lehman. Based on the play Sabrina Fair *by Samuel Taylor. Director of photography, Charles Lang, Jr. Music by Frederick Hollander. Film editor, Arthur Schmidt. Assistant director, C. C. Coleman, Jr. Art directors, Hal Pereira and Walter Tyler. Set decorations by Sam Comer and Ray Moyer. Costumes by Edith Head. Makeup artist, Wally Westmore. Special effects by John P. Fulton and Farciot Edouart. Sound recorders, Harold Lewis and John Cope. Running time, 113 minutes.*

CAST

Linus Larrabee	HUMPHREY BOGART
Sabrina Fairchild	AUDREY HEPBURN
David Larrabee	WILLIAM HOLDEN
Oliver Larrabee	Walter HAMPDEN
Thomas Fairchild	John WILLIAMS
Elizabeth Tyson	Martha HYER
Gretchen Van Horn	Joan VOHS
Baron	Marcel Dalio
The Professor	Marcel Hillaire
Maude Larrabee	Nella Walker
Mr. Tyson	Francis X. Bushman
Miss McCardle	Ellen Corby

SYNOPSIS

Sabrina Fairchild, daughter of the chauffeur to the wealthy Larrabee family, falls in love with David Larrabee, the family's younger son, but David sees her only as a moonstruck adolescent. After trying to commit suicide with the exhausts of eight automobiles in the Larrabee garage, Sabrina is packed off to Paris by her father to prepare herself for a job as a cook.

After two years in Paris, Sabrina returns with a French wardrobe and a dissatisfaction with her status as a chauffeur's daughter. She sets out to marry David, who now sees her as the beautiful and worldly-wise young lady she has become. David, however, is engaged to Elizabeth Tyson, whose connections will be useful to the Larrabee enterprises, and the family is determined that nothing shall interfere with the marriage.

Particularly concerned is old Oliver Larrabee, whose life burden is getting the last olive out of bottles and into martinis. David's austere older brother, Linus, a methodical and somewhat stuffy businessman, decides to distract Sabrina from her crush on David by courting her himself. Oliver is dubious and hopes that Linus remembers how to act with a girl, but Linus assures him that it will all come back, that it's just like riding a bicycle. He sets out in a now-tight Yale sweater and

With Audrey Hepburn

equipped with a phonograph that plays only one record, "Yes, We Have No Bananas."

Linus' diversionary tactics are interrupted by the task of devising a special hammock for his playboy brother, whose posterior is damaged after sitting on the champagne glasses he carries in his hip pockets. Linus' courtship ends in unexpected triumph, for he falls in love with the charming Sabrina and marries her himself.

With Walter Hampden,
Nella Walker, and
William Holden

With William Holden

With Warren Stevens, Mari Alden, and Edmond O'Brien

The Barefoot Contessa
1954

A Figaro Incorporated Production. Released thru United Artists. Color by Technicolor. Directed by Joseph L. Mankiewicz. Original screenplay by Joseph L. Mankiewicz. Production supervisor, Forrest E. Johnston. Production associates, Franco Magli and Michael Waszynski. Director of photography, Jack Cardiff. Music by Mario Nascimbene. Film editor, William Hornbeck. Assistant director, Pietro Mussetta. Art director, Arrigo Equini. Gowns by Fontana. Sound recorder, Charles Knott. Running time, 128 minutes.

CAST

Harry Dawes	HUMPHREY BOGART
Maria Vargas	AVA GARDNER
Oscar Muldoon	Edmond O'BRIEN
Alberto Bravano	Marius GORING
Eleanora Torlato-Favrini	Valentina CORTESA
Vincenzo Torlato-Favrini	Rossano BRAZZI
Jerry	Elizabeth Sellars
Kirk Edwards	Warren Stevens
Pedro	Franco Interlenghi
Myrna	Mari Aldon
Mrs. Eubanks	Bessie Love
Drunken Blonde	Diana Decker
J. Montague Brown	Bill Fraser
Night Club Proprietor	Alberto Rabagliati
Busboy	Enzo Staiola
Maria's Mother	Haria Zanoli
Maria's Father	Renato Chiantoni
Mr. Black	John Parrish
Mr. Blue	Jim Gerald
Gypsy Dancer	Riccardo Rioli
The Pretender	Tonio Selwart
The Pretender's Wife	Margaret Anderson
Lulu McGee	Gertrude Flynn
Hector Eubanks	John Horne
Eddie Blake	Robert Christopher
Chambermaid	Anna Maria Paduan
Chauffeur	Carlo Dale

With Ava Gardner

With Elizabeth Sellers

With Edmond O'Brien
and Warren Stevens

With Elizabeth Sellers
and Edmond O'Brien

With Rossano Brazzi
and Valentina Cortesa

With Rossano Brazzi
and Ava Gardner

SYNOPSIS

Harry Dawes, a washed-up movie director, is hired by Kirk Edwards, a rich boor, to write and direct a film calling for a glamorous woman. Talent-scouting in Europe, they go to a Madrid cabaret to see a dancer Kirk has been told about, Maria Vargas. Maria likes Harry as immediately as she dislikes Kirk, and she agrees to make the picture in Rome. Maria becomes a star overnight, and Harry's career itself attains a new luster; their relationship becomes one of deep friendship.

With his script girl, Jerry, with whom he is in love, Harry goes to a party given by Kirk for millionaire Alberto Bravano. Bravano openly admires Maria, whom he takes for Kirk's mistress, and invites her to join his Riviera yachting party. When Kirk forbids her to go, she accepts, and press agent Oscar Muldoon, tired of stooging for Kirk, jumps at the opportunity to switch his allegiance to Bravano. Bravano discovers, as Kirk had, that Maria is untouchable by men of his type, but he enjoys knowing that people assume she is his.

One evening as Bravano is gambling at a casino, Maria takes some of his chips and cashes them, throwing the money from a window to her gypsy lover. When Bravano loses, he accuses Maria of bringing him bad luck. Count Vincenzo Torlato-Favrini, who has witnessed the scene at the window, slaps Bravano and escorts Maria from the casino. Maria goes to stay at the Count's palazzo with Vincenzo and his sister, Eleanora. She falls in love with Vincenzo and he asks her to marry him. At the wedding, Harry gives the bride away.

On a rainy night months later, Maria comes to Harry's hotel room and tells him of her wedding night —how, really in love at last, she had found her husband impotent, the result of a war wound. But she will make Vincenzo happy—she is going to have a baby. This will perpetuate his family line, which, she believes, is what he wants; he will come to love the child as his own. Harry warns her that the opposite is true, that Vincenzo is a proud man finishing life on his own terms, but Maria insists she knows better.

As Maria leaves, Harry sees Vincenzo's car follow hers. Harry follows them to the palazzo, and as he arrives hears two shots from the direction of the servants' quarters. Vincenzo appears, carrying the limp body of Maria. He tells Harry that Maria is dead and so is the man. They go into the house. Calmly, Vincenzo notifies the police.

With Leo G. Carroll and
Basil Rathbone

With Peter Ustinov and
Aldo Ray

We're No Angels
1955

A Paramount Picture. In VistaVision. Color by Technicolor. Directed by Michael Curtiz. Produced by Pat Duggan. Screenplay by Ranald MacDougall. Based on the play La Cuisine des Anges *by Albert Husson. Director of photography, Loyal Griggs. Music by Frederick Hollander. Film editor, Arthur Schmidt. Assistant director, John Coonan. Dialogue assistant, Norman Stuart. Art directors, Hal Pereira and Roland Anderson. Set decorations by Sam Comer and Grace Gregory. Costumes by Mary Grant. Makeup artist, Wally Westmore. Special effects by John P. Fulton. Sound recorders, Hugo Grenzbach and John Cope. Songs: "Sentimental Moments" by Frederick Hollander and Ralph Freed; "Ma France Bien-Aimée" by G. Martini and* Roger Wagner. Color consultant, Richard Mueller. Running time, 103 minutes.

CAST

Joseph	HUMPHREY BOGART
Albert	ALDO RAY
Jules	PETER USTINOV
Amelie Ducotel	Joan BENNETT
Andre Trochard	Basil RATHBONE
Felix Ducotel	Leo G. CARROLL
Paul Trochard	John Baer
Isabelle Ducotel	Gloria Talbott
Madame Parole	Lea Penman
Arnaud	John Smith

With Leo G. Carroll

SYNOPSIS

Joseph, a forger-embezzler-con man; Albert, a slow-witted murderer; and Jules, a safecracker with a weakness for manslaughter, escape from Devil's Island on Christmas Eve. Anxious to shed their prison garb, they descend on a dry goods store, intending to steal civilian clothes. They are discovered by the shopkeeper, Felix Ducotel, his wife, Amelie, and their daughter, Isabelle, who take them for parolee carpenters, come to repair their leaky roof. Befriended by the family, the convicts are won over by their kindness and decide not to rob and murder them, agreeing that "cutting their throats might spoil their Christmas."

They find the family menaced by André Trochard, a tyrannical, avaricious relative who owns the store and who has come from Paris to inspect the books, which the bumbling Ducotel has never been able to balance. Isabelle fancies herself in love with André's nephew, Paul, a foppish cad whose heart, too, is full of love, but only for himself. Melted by the pitiful incompetence of the honest Ducotels, the convicts find themselves playing Santa Claus.

Joseph sells an ill-fitting coat to a befuddled customer, and collects a delinquent account from a protesting matron. The genial trio further bolsters the family's sagging spirits with a turkey and a Christmas tree—both, of course, stolen. The best Christmas present of all comes when the greedy Trochard insists on seizing a basket containing Albert's pet viper, whose bite sends him quickly to his reward. Paul meets a similar fate while picking the pockets of his dead uncle.

When Arnaud, a handsome young ship's doctor, comes to make out the death certificates, the convicts commandeer the boy to woo Isabelle. Bidding farewell to the Ducotels, the three jovial thugs find themselves homesick for prison and decide to return to Devil's Island, confident that they can escape whenever they wish.

With Aldo Ray, Peter Ustinov, Gloria Talbott, and John Smith

With Lee J. Cobb

The Left Hand of God

1955

A 20th Century-Fox Picture. CinemaScope. Color by DeLuxe. Directed by Edward Dmytryk. Produced by Buddy Adler. Screenplay by Alfred Hayes. Based on the novel by William E. Barrett. Director of photography, Franz Planer. Music by Victor Young. Film editor, Dorothy Spencer. Assistant director, Ben Kadish. Art directors, Lyle Wheeler and Maurice Ransford. Set decorations by Walter M. Scott and Frank Wade. Wardrobe director, Charles Le Maire. Costumes by Travilla. Makeup artist, Ben Nye. Hair styles by Helen Turpin. Special effects by Ray Kellogg. Sound recorders, Eugene Grossman and Harry M. Leonard.

Orchestrations by Leo Shuken and Sidney Cutner. Color consultant, Leonard Doss. Technical adviser, Frank Tang. Running time, 87 minutes.

CAST

Jim Carmody	HUMPHREY BOGART
Anne Scott	GENE TIERNEY
Mieh Yang	LEE J. COBB
Beryl Sigman	Agnes Moorehead
Dr. David Sigman	E. G. Marshall
Mary Yin	Jean Porter
Reverend Cornelius	Carl Benton Reid
John Wong	Victor Sen Yung
Jan Teng	Philip Ahn
Chun Tien	Benson Fong
Father O'Shea	Richard Cutting
Pao Ching	Leon Lontoc
Father Keller	Don Forbes
Woman in Sarong	Noel Toy
Feng Tso Lin	Peter Chong
Woman in Kimono	Marie Tsien
The Boy	Stephen Wong
Celeste	Sophie Chin
Li Kwan	George Chan
Hospital Orderly	Walter Soo Hoo
Orderly	Henry S. Quan
Nurse	Doris Chung
Old Man	Moy Ming
Mi Lu	George Lee
Father	Beal Wong
Pao Chu	Stella Lynn
Reverend Marvin	Robert Burton
Midwife	Soo Yong

With Gene Tierney

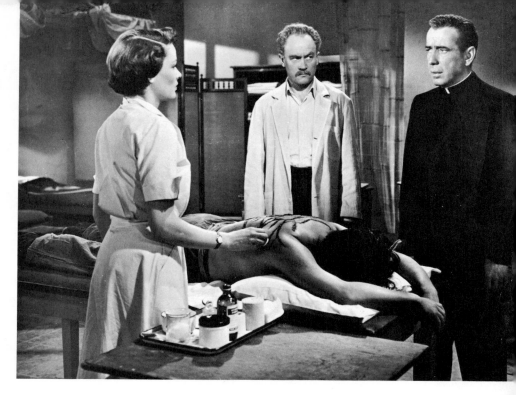

With Gene Tierney
and E. G. Marshall

SYPNOSIS

Jim Carmody, an American flyer forced down in China during World War II, has cast his lot with Mieh Yang, a Chinese war lord who saved him from his wrecked plane and made him his "military adviser." During a raid Yang's men kill a priest, and Carmody, angered by the wanton murder and restless after three years with Yang, escapes in the dead priest's clothing. Learning that the priest was en route to St. Mary's Mission to replace a priest who has died, Carmody makes his way to the mission and introduces himself as the replacement. He meets David Sigman, the mission's doctor, his wife Beryl, and Anne Scott, a nurse.

Ushered almost immediately into his priestly duties, Carmody carries off the impersonation with some help from the mission library and a good deal of luck. He finds himself attracted to Anne and she to him, but they suppress their feelings, Carmody from necessity, Anne from feelings of guilt over her attraction to a "priest." Carmody takes his problem to Reverend Marvin, a minister in a distant village, who advises him to write the Bishop a complete account of his actions. Carmody composes the letter, which Marvin dispatches by courier.

Returning to his mission, Carmody finds the village

With Gene Tierney, E. G. Marshall,
and Agnes Moorehead

With E. G. Marshall

With Carl Benton Reid and Don Forbes

in confusion over the approach of Yang and his bandits. The Sigmans and Anne propose organizing a fighting force, but Carmody tells them that Yang is here for him, not for the poor loot of the village. Yang enters the village, determined to bring the deserter back to his troops. Carmody offers to gamble with Yang for his services against the safety of the village. Twice they throw dice, and Carmody wins both times. Yang takes his loss with good grace and withdraws his troops.

The next day a caravan arrives bringing Father Cornelius, the Bishop's representative, in response to Carmody's letter. Father Cornelius sends Carmody to the Bishop to tell his story and make his penance to the church for his masquerade. Although Father Cornelius refuses to let Anne talk to Carmody before his departure, he lets Anne know that if she follows on the next caravan, she will be free to join the man she has come to love.

With Lee J. Cobb

With Fredric March and Dewey Martin

With Dewey Martin

The Desperate Hours

1955

A Paramount Picture. In VistaVision. Produced and directed by William Wyler. Associate producer, Robert Wyler. Screenplay by Joseph Hayes, based on his novel and play. Director of photography, Lee Garmes. Music by Gail Kubik. Film editor, Robert Swink. Assistant director, C. C. Coleman, Jr. Art directors, Hal Pereira and Joseph MacMillan Johnson. Set decorations by Sam Comer and Grace Gregory. Costumes by Edith Head. Makeup artist, Wally Westmore. Special effects by John P. Fulton and Farciot Edouart. Sound recorders, Hugo Grenzbach and Winston Leverett. Running time, 112 minutes.

With Fredric March, Richard Eyer,
and Martha Scott

CAST

Glenn Griffin	HUMPHREY BOGART
Dan Hilliard	FREDRIC MARCH
Jesse Bard	Arthur KENNEDY
Eleanor Hilliard	Martha SCOTT
Hal Griffin	Dewey MARTIN
Chuck	Gig YOUNG
Cindy Hilliard	Mary MURPHY
Ralphie Hilliard	Richard Eyer
Sam Kobish	Robert Middleton
Detective	Alan Reed
Winston	Bert Freed
Masters	Ray Collins
Carson	Whit Bissell
Fredericks	Ray Teal
Detective	Michael Moore
Detective	Don Haggerty
Sal	Ric Roman
Dutch	Pat Flaherty
Miss Swift	Beverly Garland
Bucky Walling	Louis Lettieri
Mrs. Walling	Ann Doran
Patterson	Walter Baldwin

SYNOPSIS

Three escaped convicts—Glenn Griffin, his brother Hal, and Sam Kobish—gunpoint their way to temporary refuge in the suburban home of a middle-class family. Hostages in their own house are Dan Hilliard, his wife, Eleanor, their daughter, Cindy, and their young son, Ralphie. To avoid suspicion, Cindy is allowed to date her fiancé, Chuck, and Dan goes to his office, but neither dares speak of his predicament for fear of endangering the lives of the others. At first thought a coward by his son, Dan recovers from his initial fright and by courage and wisdom acts to defeat the invaders. Chuck meanwhile, suspicious of Cindy's strange behavior, goes to Deputy Sheriff Jesse Bard, who surrounds the house with police.

Hal decides to take his chances by fleeing. While he and Griffin are outside the house, Dan slams a door on Kobish's arm, seizes his gun, and forces him outside, where he is caught in police searchlights and killed. Finding that Ralphie has conducted an escape on his own and has been caught by Griffin, Dan offers to help Griffin with the police if Ralphie is released. Griffin lets the boy go, and Dan calls for him to run, knowing that Griffin's gun is unloaded. Dan orders Griffin from the house, but outside, Griffin makes a break for freedom, and the police shoot him down.

With Fredric March and Robert Middleton

With Robert Middleton, Richard Eyer,
Fredric March, Martha Scott, and
Mary Murphy

187

With Nehemiah Persoff,
Jan Sterling and
Rod Steiger

The Harder They Fall

1956

*A Columbia Picture. Directed by Mark Robson. Pro-
duced by Philip Yordan. Screenplay by Philip Yordan.
Based on the novel by Budd Schulberg. Director of
photography, Burnett Guffey. Music by Hugo Fried-
hofer. Film editor, Jerome Thoms. Assistant director,
Milton Feldman. Art director, William Flannery. Set
decorations by William Kiernan and Alfred E. Spencer.
Makeup artist, Clay Campbell. Hair styles by Helen
Hunt. Sound recorder, Lambert Day. Orchestrations by
Arthur Morton. Musical director, Lionel Newman.
Technical adviser, John Indrisano. Running time, 109
minutes.*

With Rod Steiger

CAST

Eddie Willis	HUMPHREY BOGART
Nick Benko	Rod STEIGER
Beth Willis	Jan STERLING
Toro Moreno	Mike Lane
Buddy Brannen	Max Baer
George	Jersey Joe Walcott
Jim Weyerhause	Edward Andrews
Art Leavitt	Harold J. Stone
Luis Agrandi	Carlos Montalban
Leo	Nehemiah Persoff
Vince Fawcett	Felice Orlandi
Max	Herbie Faye
Danny McKeogh	Rusty Lane
Pop	Jack Albertson
Frank	Val Avery
Tommy	Tommy Herman
Joey	Vinnie DeCarlo
Gus Dundee	Pat Comiskey
Sailor Rigazzo	Matt Murphy
Chief Firebird	Abel Fernandez
Alice	Marion Carr

With Mike Lane, Rusty Lane,
Jersey Joe Walcott, Rod Steiger,
Nehemiah Persoff, and Felice Orlandi

SYNOPSIS

Nick Benko, head of a fight-promotion syndicate, imports an Argentinian giant named Toro Moreno, who looks formidable but actually has "a powder-puff punch and a glass jaw." To publicize the freak battler, Benko hires Eddie Willis, an ex-sports columnist, who accepts the job despite the misgivings of his wife, Beth.

Fixing fight after fight, Benko eventually gets Toro a match with Gus Dundee, the ex-champ, but Dundee, having taken severe punishment from Buddy Brannen in his previous fight, collapses in the ring and dies of a brain hemorrhage. Thinking he has killed him, Toro refuses to appear in the title bout until Willis reveals the series of fixes to him.

Determined to stick it out in order to take money home to his parents, Toro goes into the ring with Brannen and takes a terrible beating, but when Willis goes to Benko to collect Toro's winnings, he is told that the giant has earned only $49.07. Outraged and disgusted, Willis gives Toro his own share, $26,000, and puts him on a plane for Argentina. Despite threats from Benko, Willis determines to write a series of articles to expose the syndicate and to get boxing outlawed in the United States "if it takes an act of Congress to do it."

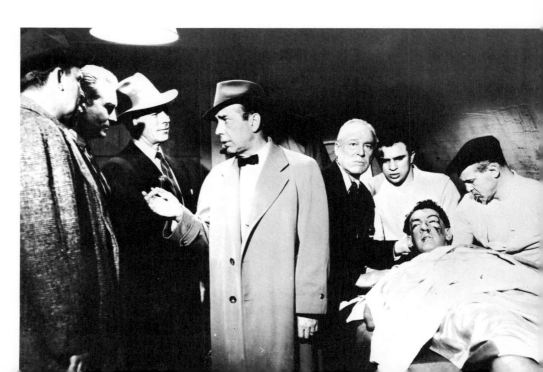

With Mike Lane

The Face of Bogey

"He was endowed with the greatest gift a man can have—talent. The whole world came to recognize it . . . His life, though not a long one measured in years, was a rich, full life . . . We have no reason to feel any sorrow for him—only for ourselves for having lost him. He is quite irreplaceable. There will never be another like him."

JOHN HUSTON